A Marriage of
CONVENIENCE

THE SIGNIFICANCE OF STABLE US-CHINA RELATIONS AND HOW THEY WILL SHAPE GLOBAL EVENTS IN THE TWENTY-FIRST CENTURY

MIKE BERDELA

Laurel,
thank you so much for
supporting a great cause.
Enjoy!

Mike

Written for American service members killed in support of Operation Iraqi Freedom and Operation Enduring Freedom—Afghanistan

100 percent of book proceeds will be donated to Hire Heroes USA (www.hireheroesusa.org) Hire Heroes is an organization started by Marine Corps veteran and former UFC fighter Brian Stann that helps transitioning service members find viable employment after separating from the military.

CONTENTS

Chapter 1

SETTING THE STAGE

As a junior in high school, I flew from Pennsylvania to Tampa, Florida, to visit my uncle COL William "Buddy" Rizzio, a Marine Corps Intelligence Officer in Central Command (CENTCOM). As a wide-eyed teenager with aspirations to attend The Citadel and follow in his footsteps to the US Marines, we spent a considerable amount of time talking about military topics as I tried to absorb as much as I could from this career military officer. Throughout our dialogue, there was an idea he strongly affirmed that confounded me at the time yet has remained with me to this day: he told me to learn Mandarin and study China, for these would be critical skills to possess in the future. At the time (several months after 9/11), the eyes of the world were on the United States' effort to dismantle the Taliban and install democracy in Afghanistan, so economic developments in China were a relative blip on the geopolitical radar. Furthermore, China's economy in 2002 wasn't even the size of France's, so his assertion struck me as an odd one since I knew that France wasn't a global or even a regional power. I just let the comment pass and didn't give it much thought since there was so much cognitive dissonance between what he was saying and what I *thought* I knew. Little did I know how right he was and that, a decade and a half later, I'd be writing a book about the importance of China.

As of this book's writing, it is evident that the world has become a vastly different place, a place my uncle had the keen foresight to envision. It seems laughable to make the Franco-Sino comparison now, as China's economy has become fully *four times* the size of France's. Never has a nation upended the global economic order at such pace (and without much notice), since from 2001 until recently, the United States was tied up in the quagmire of dual Middle East wars and had to deal with the "Great Recession" of 2007–9. In 2011, the Obama administration rightly commenced a concerted rebalancing of our political and military focus eastward in what was deemed the United States' "Pivot to Asia." The pivot was based on the assertion that the dominant issues of the twenty-first century will likely be decided in the Asia-Pacific region, where the United States will be a primary actor as it (hopefully) disengages militarily from the Middle East.

For the previous seventy years, global events had been shaped and framed in a post–World War II system dominated by a Western-centric order, led foremost by the United States. The United Nations, the International Monetary Fund, the World Bank, the World Trade Organization, NATO, and US dollar hegemony were some of the vehicles used by the United States and the West to cement and solidify this order. During this time, the most important transnational relationship was between the USSR and the United States—the two entities that garnered most of the spoils from that great conflict. The world was divided between East and West, communist and capitalist, Warsaw Pact and NATO. Each side knew the other well, and through the policy of Mutual Assured Destruction (MAD), there was some semblance of stability between these two belligerents.

With the Soviet Union's collapse in 1991, the United States enjoyed a seminal moment of unchallenged hegemony. However, with the rise of trade and globalization, and the modernization of developing nations (especially China), power dynamics have been rapidly changing. The sudden increase in trade between the United States and China over the past few decades (currently totaling close to $600 billion annually), coupled with China's military modernization, which threatens to shake the current order in Asia, are just a few of the reasons why this relationship is significant.[1] Also relevant is the fact that China's perpetual 10 percent annual growth has allowed it to leapfrog the world's largest economies with breakneck speed, surpassing not only France, but also the United Kingdom, Germany, and Japan—all within the past fifteen years.[2] The single greatest economic and foreign policy issue of my generation will be the rebalancing of economic power from the "Old Guard" (Europe/Japan) to the new competitor (China). The United States will be in a holding pattern as the world's sole hyperpower for the near term, but estimates based on current trends by the International Monetary Fund (IMF) have China surpassing the United States economically sometime in the mid-2020s.

In just under one hundred pages, this book will address the symbiotic, sometimes tense, and oft-misunderstood relationship between the United States and China. This partnership is an indispensable component of global economics and trade, regional politics in Asia, and (increasingly) security and military endeavors. The crux of this book's argument is that China and the United States are inextricably linked, and a tacit policy of Mutual Assured *Economic* Destruction will be the primary driver that normalizes this bilateral relationship. Our nations' economies are intertwined in such a profound manner that there would be no victors in a potential battle; any gains would be nominal and Pyrrhic in nature—a fact that should guide policymakers on both sides and ensure stable relations. This book will supply requisite amounts of detail, statistics, and figures to fully explain this matter yet will refrain from using much esoteric vernacular so that even the casual foreign policy observer would not be lost. This book won't make readers experts in the field, but it will vastly enhance their knowledge of several key US-Sino relations topics, of which they likely possess only vague familiarity via fleeting mention on network news. Dispassionate facts are the bedrock of this book, and I will use as little inference and induction as possible. To that aim, I have included more than thirty charts/ tables and an excess of one hundred nonpartisan sources that provide scholarly weight to my arguments.

The reader will also notice that economics is my primary concern with regards to US-Sino relations. Economics is foreign policy's center of gravity, as geopolitical and military clout must always be backed by a strong and stable economy. Outliers have swum against this current, but they invariably end in collapse. For example, for almost fifty years, the USSR had an extremely robust and aggressive military and foreign policy apparatus, even though it lagged far behind the United States in economic development. In fact, it could be argued that its military strength was superior to ours (in raw numbers, not technologically), as it spent upward of 20 percent of its GDP on defense during the Cold War—a number that proved unsustainable and hastened its downfall. Paradoxically, excess defense spending makes a country weaker and it is generally accepted that military expenditures should encompass only between 2 and 4 percent of GDP. Anything above that threshold is considered excessive, as it siphons money from other areas that could help expand GDP. As the chart shows, at the time of their collapse, the Soviets had almost forty thousand serviceable nuclear weapons, almost *double* what the Americans had, and by the late 1980s, they had increased defense spending to an astronomical 27 percent of GDP.[3] By this point, their economy was in the midst of a prolonged period of stagnation that a strong military could not mask.

Chart 1
US AND USSR/RUSSIA's NUCLEAR WEAPONS COUNT, 1945–2010

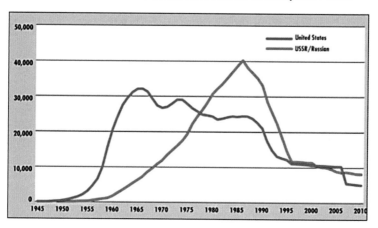

In summation, this book will answer four distinct questions in order to give readers a broad sense of historical grounding and contemporary context so they may fully grasp the nature and importance of this relationship.

1. How did this marriage of convenience come about? (chapters 2,3)
2. What does the current power dynamic look like? (chapters 4,5)
3. Are these nations friends, foes, or something different altogether? (chapters 6,7)
4. What will this marriage look like in the future? (chapters 8, 9)

BEFORE MOVING TO CHAPTER 2, take a minute to read the following, as it will afford you a comprehensive set of definitions that may be familiar only to those who have spent time studying foreign policy.

globalization: The increase in international commerce and the lowering of tariffs and protectionist policies. Globalization has created an interconnected global economy whereby the diffusion and cross-pollination of people, products, and ideas across borders has made the world smaller. Sometimes used as a pejorative, globalization is often viewed as the culprit behind outsourcing and Western companies producing products overseas at a lower cost.

National power statuses:

• A *hyperpower* is the lone dominating state in a unipolar world. Since the fall of the USSR in 1991, the United States has fallen into this category.

• A *superpower* is a state that is clearly more powerful than almost all other countries, especially in a bipolar world (for example, the United States and the USSR during the Cold War). At present, the European Union (EU) satisfies this requirement when it acts with one voice, as does China (primarily in the economic realm).

• A *great power* is a state that is one of the leading powers in the world and has the ability to extend its reach globally. Germany, Japan, and the United Kingdom are considered contemporary great powers.

• A *regional power* is the center of gravity in its region but does not yet have global influence. India, Brazil, and South Africa are current examples.

• A *middle power* is a state that cannot dominate others but may still be modern and industrialized (Canada).

Gross Domestic Product (GDP): GDP is the sum of all the goods and services produced by a nation in a given year. In simple terms, it is the economic size of a nation.

Note: There are two ways to measure GDP: nominal terms and purchasing power parity (PPP) terms. Nominal GDP simply uses currency exchange rates (to the US dollar) in order to standardize the economic size of one nation to the next, while PPP GDP uses a system whereby the purchasing power of a currency is compared to the cost of purchasing local goods. I use nominal GDP throughout this book because it gives the reader a better sense of the economic strength of the *nation* at large, whereby PPP gives a better assessment of economic strength at the *local* level.

Bretton Woods economic system: Named after the meeting location of the World War II victors in Bretton Woods, New Hampshire, in 1944, this new global economic system was created at the summit and reigns supreme to this day. It is anchored by the US dollar, the IMF, the World Bank, and the primacy of capitalism and free trade.

the West: "The West" is a subjective and fluid term, yet for this book, it refers to the modern, industrialized, capitalist, and democratic nations that have been culturally and economically dominant for the past few centuries. In a historical context, Western nations were typically classified as white, Christian, Democratic, and English speaking. When I use this term here, I am referring to the United States, Europe, Canada, Australia, New Zealand, and Japan. Although ethnically and culturally different from the rest, Japan is included because of its modern economy and liberal democratic and capitalist system.

emerging markets: These are former third-world nations that have been rapidly rising as a result of globalization and trade. Dozens of nations fall into this category, yet when I mention emerging markets or industrializing nations, I am referring primarily to the BRICS nations (Brazil, Russia, India, China, South Africa), along with Argentina, Indonesia, Iran, Korea, Mexico, Turkey, and Saudi Arabia.

International Monetary Fund (IMF) and the World Bank: The fund's focus is to stabilize exchange rates and balance the international financial system, while the bank deals with developmental projects, poverty reduction, and providing loans to low-income nations. Combined, the World Bank and the IMF are the twin intergovernmental pillars that support the structure of the world's economic and financial order.

United Nations Security Council: Comprising the five major World War II victors, the UN Security Council is the primary forum for settling and debating international disputes. The five veto-wielding permanent members are China, France, Great Britain, Russia, and the United States.

Chapter 2

THE RISE OF THE UNITED STATES AND CHINA'S CENTURY OF HUMILIATION

America and China took very distinct routes to achieve their contemporary statuses as global economic powers. We will begin this chapter by discussing America's rise. America became the world's largest economy in the 1890s (dethroning Great Britain in the process), owed in large part to its vast quantities of natural resources, an entrepreneurial and productive workforce, clearly defined rule of law, and effective governance.[1] In retrospect, it is evident that America was destined to be a world power because of two profound advantages it held over its peers: a dominant geographic position and the ability to assimilate immigrant labor.

First, its location is such that an invasion by a belligerent power is not only unlikely but also almost impossible. Flanked by the largesse of the Atlantic and Pacific Oceans, the United States enjoys the benefits of geographic-based strategic depth for the simple fact that any invading fleet would be identified and compromised well in advance. Having Canada and Mexico on its borders also decreases the risk of a land-borne invasion for many geographic, economic, and political reasons. An assault from the north would be highly unlikely, as its northern neighbor, Canada, is sparsely populated, mostly barren (upward of 90 percent of the country is uninhabitable), and is littered with natural barriers and mountains.

To the south, Mexico is a comparatively weaker neighbor, and after concluding their border skirmishes, it became more aligned with US interests. It is America's third-largest trading partner and has a growing cultural connection owing to the increasing Latin population in the States.[2] Mexico also enjoys many ancillary benefits by being in such proximity to a hyperpower, making it unlikely that it would be sympathetic to invading nations attempting to use it as a staging ground for a United States-destined assault. Those two benefits (weak neighbors to the north/south and large oceans to the east/west) offered the United States unique advantages, allowing it to grow its economy unabated by the prospect of war while the European powers (Britain, France, Portugal, Spain, Austria-Hungary, the Dutch, and unified Germany) had to contest and toil for control of land and treasure—combined, these European lands were roughly half the size of the United States, showing how the propensity for conflict and war in a limited area was an inescapable issue.

While its location provided geopolitical shelter to grow without the prospect of invasion, its priority for openness, tolerance, and large-scale immigration was the economic engine behind its rise—a recipe frequently used by hyperpowers in the past.

To be globally dominant, a society must be at the forefront of the world's technological, military, and economic development. And at any given historical moment, the most valuable human capital is never to be found in any one locale or within any one ethnic or religious group. To pull away from its rivals on a global sale, a society must pull into itself the world's best and brightest, regardless of ethnicity, religion, or background. This is what every hyperpower in history has done, from Achaemenid Persia to the Great Mongol Empire to the British Empire, and the way they have done it is through tolerance. The United States implemented this policy wholesale; between 1820 and 1914, more than thirty million people poured into the country—the largest human migration in world history.[3]

Centuries of war (but particularly the two world wars) left Europe tired of conquest, broke, and unable/unwilling to further its colonial ambitions. America, by contrast, was now primed to enter its zenith on the world stage: its mainland was untouched by battle, it was the world's biggest creditor, it had a dynamic and entrepreneurial economy, and it held two-thirds of global gold reserves.[4] The aftermath of these two wars thrust America into a position it was not comfortable dealing with at the time—namely that of global hegemon. As the only industrial giant left standing, it financed the war-torn countries of Europe back to health through its Marshall Plan. Yet from its inception, the United States was not fond of international affairs, evident by the following declarations and actions by former US presidents and leaders.

At his farewell address, President George Washington stated that it was not a good idea to create "permanent alliances with any portion of the foreign world" and that commerce with other nations should be maintained, although there should not be involvement in European wars and no entering into any "entangling" alliances.[5]

In 1823, President James Monroe advocated staying out of foreign conflict in what is now known as the Monroe Doctrine, saying, "In the wars of the European powers, in matters relating to themselves, we have never taken part, nor does it comport with our policy, so to do. It is only when our rights are invaded, or seriously menaced that we resent injuries, or make preparations for our defense."[6]

In 1916, President Woodrow Wilson won reelection by highlighting his non-interventionist record; "he kept us out of the war" was his supporters' rallying cry. In 1919, a band of mostly Republican senators known as the "Irreconcilables" blocked the ratification of the Treaty of Versailles and entrance to the League of Nations (the precursor to the United Nations). Without the world's largest economy party to the league, it was toothless and set the conditions for World War II as fascist regimes in Germany, Italy, and Japan invaded their neighbors without any threat of reprisal.

During the onset of World War II, the United States abstained as long as it could yet still supplied Britain with loans and equipment under the Lend Lease Act. It was then compelled to enter after Pearl Harbor—a full two years after Hitler commenced his polices of *Anschluss* (Annexation) and *Lebensraum* (Living Space) on Central Europe.

The United States' reluctance in the foreign policy arena made it an unlikely and unwilling candidate to take the mantle from any of the European powers after World War II, yet this role was unanimously bestowed on it at war's end. Britain shared with the United States a common white, Anglo-Saxon, Protestant (WASP) heritage and ancestry and felt comfortable ceding its position as the de facto global hegemon to a nation that it felt would act much as it had during its reign. The two countries tacitly agreed to the "Special Relationship" (an oft-mentioned term during the Reagan-Thatcher era), which essentially meant that Great Britain would publicly support policies advocated by the United States, and in reciprocation, the United States would provide the British with a seat at the table to confer on international issues. British support instantly infused American policy with international legitimacy, which it needed, as it was an adolescent nation without much pedigree in the arena. Although Britain ceded most of its empire after World War II, the queen ceremonially maintained her position as the head of state for the Commonwealth of Nations (formerly called the British Commonwealth), which consists of fifty-three nations and 2.3 billion citizens, amounting to almost one-third of the global population.[7] For this reason, the tiny island nation of England is still a major player in world affairs, as it continues to "punch above its weight" globally and has the United States' ear to offer counsel and advice. The relevancy of the "Special Relationship" was on display during the lead-up to the invasion of Iraq in 2003, whereby Prime Minister Blair was coaxed (some say prodded) into supporting the failed American-led operation, causing him to lose reelection. Even though it was ultimately voted down in the UN Security Council, the mission, primarily due to Britain's support, was instantly stamped with some semblance of international legitimacy.

While Great Britain facilitated a smooth transition to a United States–led order in the political arena, the 1944 Bretton Woods system did so with respect to economics. Bretton Woods established several systems that solidified the United States' position as the driver of global economics, namely the IMF, World Bank, and the use of the "greenback" (the US dollar) as the world's reserve currency. As the only large Western economy left unscathed with the requisite systems in place to be the anchor for political and economic stability, the United States was the only real option to lead these organizations. The IMF and World Bank's function is to monitor exchange rates, lend currency to nations with trade deficits, encourage and further international trade, and lend money to war-torn and poor nations. The fact that these loans were typically denominated in dollars solidified the fact that the global economy's health would be dependent on a vibrant American economy, and it would be in all nations' interests to keep the US currency and economy healthy.

Whereas World War II cemented America's place in the global world order, China's "Century of Humiliation," from the mid-1800s to mid-1900s, left it with enduring national scars that frame its modern-day outlook. This timeframe was characterized by unprovoked Western and Japanese military incursions into China's homeland, against which it was embarrassingly powerless to defend. To understand the gravity and long-lasting psychological impact from these wars, we must first understand the impressive nature and historical context of Chinese culture, strength, and power. For much of its more than four-thousand-year civilization, China had a socially cohesive, prosperous, and dynamic economy that was ahead of its time in many important industries, shipbuilding being a prominent example. In fact, fifteenth-century Chinese explorer Zheng He captained a number of mammoth treasure-seeking vessels several times the size of Columbus's state-of-the-art ships. These treasure ships were four hundred feet long, making them the largest wooden boats on the planet (see picture 2.1). Zheng's fleet of over three hundred ships carried over twenty-eight thousand men, an armada that dwarfed those of European explorers, often by a factor of ten or more in size, staff, and equipment. These vessels made a statement to the world about the immense strength and power of the Chinese dynasty. But it was a temporary statement shrouded in vanity and conceit, for the Chinese did not take advantage of these marvels as they conquered no territory, retained no overseas seaports, and had no want for colonial holdings.[8]

These seafaring voyages were abandoned soon after they had commenced on the grounds that they were unnecessary and superficial expenses. The Ming Dynasty's concerted policy of retreating to nativism was a factor that led to China lagging

Zheng He's treasure ship versus Christopher Columbus's *Santa Maria. http://bhoffert.faculty.noctrl.edu/HST261/21.MingRestoration.html.*

behind the West in technological advances. China was a large and prosperous kingdom, confident in its rich history and aptitude to remain self-sufficient and avoid foreign trade. Chinese exceptionalism and ethnocentrism is clearly evident in their depiction of their homeland as the "Middle Kingdom." The Chinese viewed themselves as globally central to world progress, culture, and history and had an emperor guided by a heavenly mandate to "rule all which is under heaven."[9] Expectedly, their maps placed the Chinese kingdom in the center, where it was flanked by barbarians and foreign invaders outside its walls. The first map on the following page shows China in the middle, surrounded by disparate states and tribes, while the second, called the 1602 *Kunyu Wangao Quantu* map (map of the "Myriad Countries of the World") shows China positioned in the center.[10]

It should be noted that viewing one's ethnicity/nationality as "exceptional" is not a concept unique to the Chinese; the term "American exceptionalism" has been ubiquitous in this country

Left: Map of the Middle Kingdom. *http:// lumdimsum.com/tag/ mapping-the-middle-kingdom.*

Below: The 1602 map of the Myriad Countries of the World. *http://www. learnmartialartsinchina.com/ kung-fu-school-blog/why-is- china-called-the-middle-kingdom.*

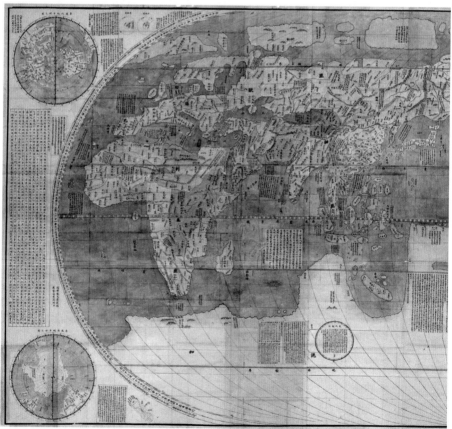

for decades. Nor is the creation of maps with one's home nation globally central an uncommon occurrence, as the British Isles were the international standard for time zones upon the system's establishment in the late nineteenth century.

While the Chinese were living behind walls and resting on their laurels as the world's largest economy, there were collections of small kingdoms and warring nobility in Europe vying to carve out their claims on the continent and across the globe. The increased competition for resources and dominions to serve under them were powerful motivators for the European powers to modernize (especially in the military realm) in order to best their fellow belligerents. They traded, exchanged ideas, made advances in the sciences, and created novel inventions, culminating in the first

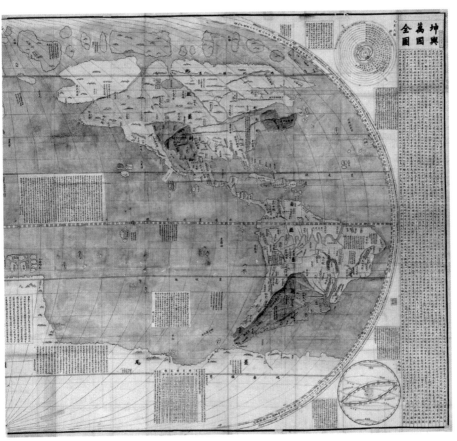

Industrial Revolution in the late eighteenth century. Although the Chinese did trade westward, they had contempt for much of the innovations being brought east, viewing British clocks and the like as nothing more than trinkets to be displayed by nobility. The lack of practical application for new ideas and inventions is one of the central reasons the Chinese fell behind the modernization curve; for example, their main use for newly discovered gunpowder was in fireworks, while the Europeans saw a much more pragmatic use for it as propellant in battle.

In order for the British to finance their nineteenth-century imperial ambitions, they needed the world's largest market (China) to be an open and solid trading partner. They specifically needed opium from the British East India company (modern-day India/Pakistan) to be exported to China's markets, yet China's dynastic leaders denied its entry. Several small skirmishes and the arrests of British traders attempting to illegally enter the mainland were the beginnings of a series of battles known as the Opium Wars, which culminated in embarrassing defeats for the Chinese. China was forced to cede Hong Kong to the British and lost dozens of its ports to foreign powers, which descended on China in order to expand their imperialist ambitions and spheres of influence.

A few decades later, China attempted to expel foreign influences and Christian missionaries from its shores in what was called the Boxer Rebellion (1899–1901). The rebels were called "boxers" by their Western enemies, who noticed their affinity for calisthenics. Eight

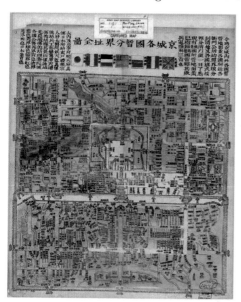

The Occupation of Beijing by Foreign Powers. *Wikimedia Commons.*

nations—Austria-Hungary, France, Italy, Germany, Japan, Russia, the United Kingdom, and the United States—allied against China in unison to quell the uprising. The rebels lost the battle, and China was forced to pay reparations, coerced to sign unequal treaties, and much of its territory was carved up and occupied by the various foreign invaders.

The Opium Wars and the Boxer Rebellion stunned the Chinese, for they had successfully battered back foreign invaders and Mongolian hordes for centuries. China's inability to galvanize its citizens and provide a cohesive defense strategy to repel the invaders was chalked up to the Qing Dynasty's inward-focused policy, as the country became unaware of the changing dynamics of the international system, technology, and war. As a response to the Qing Dynasty's inability to protect its citizens against foreign aggression, it was overthrown in 1911 via the Xinhai Revolution, when the modern-day Chinese state was born (called the Republic of China, or ROC). Over the next few decades, China warred with itself over which faction would succeed the dynastic period. This fighting culminated in the Communists winning in 1949 and establishing the People's Republic of China (PRC) as they drove the ROC government to the island of Taiwan to take refuge (where it remains to this day).

Across the Sea of Japan, the Japanese saw the awesome power that technological advances had ushered in, enabling the much smaller British and Western forces to best their Chinese

The Carving up of China: Queen Victoria (Britain), Kaiser Wilhelm II (Germany), Tsar Nicolas II (Russia), Marianne (France), and a samurai (Japan) decide how to partition China as a Chinaman helplessly watches. *Wikimedia Commons.*

23

counterparts in battle. The Japanese knew that their isolationist and feudal-based Shogunate system was starting to fall behind technologically and would be unable to repel foreign invaders—similar to China's inability to prevent incursions from imperialist powers. Therefore, a newfound nationalist sentiment spread throughout the country, whereby the Shogun dynasty was overthrown by a coup d'état and Emperor Meiji was installed as supreme leader. He then began a series of modernizations and technological advancements in what was called the Meiji Restoration. This newly motivated nation constructed an ambitious global trading network that allowed it to import vast amounts of natural resources to industrialize, modernize, and militarize—with an eye on its Chinese neighbors to the east. Japan knew that as an island nation a fraction the size of China, it could be victorious only if it had technological superiority in the field of battle.

By 1890, Japan was considered a first-rate global power as it handedly defeated China in the Sino-Japanese War and then the Russians in the Russo-Japanese War. China's Qing Dynasty lost significant prestige as Taiwan was temporarily ceded to Japan and Korea was lost as a vassal state and absorbed under the Japanese sphere of influence. The "Land of the Rising Sun" was now a full-blown imperial power, the unchallenged hegemon in Asia, and led over a regional order where China was relegated to second-rate status. The Century of Humiliation's most devastating period was the 1930s to '40s, when imperial Japan invaded and garrisoned Manchuria, commenced the "Rape of Nanking," and killed ten million Chinese throughout the war.[11]

During the Century of Humiliation, the Chinese were caught flat-footed and off guard, unaware of the changing dynamics of war, industrialization, and trade. These dynamics allowed nations they viewed as lesser powers to defeat them in the field of battle, a period of national shame the Chinese vow not to repeat in the twenty-first century. In order for the West to grasp why many Chinese have less than stellar views of those outside its borders, they must acknowledge the one-sided incursions and occupations by foreign powers that caused a proud Chinese people with a rich history to be subservient and subdued in their own homeland for over a century.

Chapter 3 will discuss how the Chinese looked to avenge this lost century with the coming to power of the Communist Party during their decades-long civil war beginning in the 1920s. It will also delve into their period of modernization and industrialization that started in earnest in the late 1970s, after the death of Mao Zedong, via their pragmatic leader Deng Xiaoping.

Chapter 3

POST WORLD WAR II CHINA

FROM MAO TO DENG

Mao Zedong was the inaugural leader of the Chinese Communist Party (CCP), besting the Nationalist Kuomintang (KMT) Party in a civil war over the right to rule the mainland in the post-dynastic era. For this reason, he is viewed as the father of modern-day China. After driving his enemies off the mainland to the island of Taiwan and forcing the South Koreans and Americans to back down to the thirty-eighth parallel during the Korean War, he was considered a national hero whose propaganda created a cult of personality akin to a deity. Yet the actual facts speak of a leader whose legacy is one of failed Communist policies and starvation on a massive scale. Mao's strict Communist economic and political ideology wiped out roughly fifty million of his citizens over his two-decade rule.[1]

The Communist Party released five-year plans starting in 1953 in order define and prioritize its national vision. Their second five-year plan (1958–63) was centered on reshaping its economy and returning prosperity and pride to a battered nation. It would accomplish this through Mao's "Great Leap Forward," a system of policies centered on collective communes of about five thousand families whereby farmers had to meet quotas for grain and steel production (the latter via backyard furnaces). Seven hundred million Chinese were placed in over twenty-six thousand communes, which provided free education and healthcare while private property and free enterprise were abolished, keeping with Communist thought.[2] Soldiers and propaganda kept order and were an enduring presence on the commune in order to affirm the greatness of Mao's polices (see pictures at right).

The intent was to make China an agricultural and industrial giant, yet it failed wholesale for several reasons. First, the steel produced in these furnaces was of poor quality, and most of it was simply tossed away when it was sent up the bureaucratic chain to be used by state-owned construction enterprises. Yet in order to keep party bosses satisfied, both the amount and quality of steel produced was inflated at all levels and created a picture of industrial success. Local Communist leaders lied about how much steel their furnace communes were creating, a practice mirrored at the provincial and regional levels, as well as among those who had Mao's ear. National steel production, along with coal,

"Great Leap Forward" propaganda: successes of the commune and strength in unity (top) and grain being sent up from the commune to be distributed among the masses (bottom). *http://www.ncas.rutgers.edu/mao-and-great-leap-forward.*

cement, and timber, was tracked and announced regularly and touted as proof of the Communist Party's ability to provide for the people. The totals had to continually increase in order to afford the party legitimacy and prevent an indictment against its rule. A second issue of the "leap" was that while many of the farmers were out looking for scrap metal for their furnaces, the elderly and the very young were left to tend the farms. Since these citizens were engaging in skill sets they had not mastered, agricultural production waned excessively. Also, whereas farmers previously had been able to grow what they wished on their farms, they were now forced to grow what the commune leaders demanded, often with disastrous results. Although exact figures are unknown, the general consensus is that forty-five million citizens died of starvation or were executed by soldiers stationed at the communes, often for the slightest infraction or not working hard enough.[3]

Even by the mid-1960s, Mao was still revered by the masses as a result of years of successful propaganda, yet there was a push among party leaders to break away from strict Communist ideals. Mao came to feel that the current party leadership in China was moving too far in a revisionist direction, with an emphasis on empirical knowledge rather than ideological purity. His own position in government had weakened after the failure of the Great Leap and the economic crisis that followed. He gathered a group of radicals to help him attack current party leadership and reassert his authority, calling it the "Cultural Revolution." The now famous *Little Red Book* of Mao's quotations was proliferated among the population, and massive purges of the "impure" elements of society (resulting in two to three million deaths) were conducted in order to revive the revolutionary spirit, which led to victory in the civil war and created the people's republic.[4] The Cultural Revolution came to an end following Mao's death in 1976, after which there was a consensus among party leaders to assign a pragmatic leader with a different vision. They chose Deng Xiaoping as a result. Although the casual observer can see that Mao was an ideologically rigid leader who oversaw decades of death, famine, and purges on a massive scale, there is a priority in remembering him in a venerable light as the father of Communist China, for if his greatness is questioned, so might be the legitimacy of the ruling Communist Party as a whole.

Deng Xiaoping famously stated that it "does not matter whether a cat is black or white, so long as it catches mice"[5]—a fresh breath of pragmatism and a noticeable departure from the ideological prison of thought evident during the Mao era. The Xiaoping regime immediately commenced an era of rapprochement and opening up of the mainland to international trade. Seeing the failures of Mao's heavy-handedness firsthand (he was imprisoned during the Cultural Revolution), Deng implemented modernization policies that were nurtured over the following decades, culminating in China's accession to the World Trade Organization (WTO) in 2001. Deng had the long-term vision of a Chinese economy that needed to shed its ideologically constrictive Communist shackles and take steps to induce capitalist and free enterprise characteristics. He knew China needed to progress from a closed economy to one where trade was encouraged and understood that malleability and openness of thought were required to make this transition.

Prior to engaging in a discussion about China's modernizations of the 1970s and onward, we must first outline basic macroeconomic tenants to supply the reader with requisite background knowledge on the subject. Economies are separated into three distinct sectors: the primary sector (agricultural), the secondary sector (manufacturing), and the tertiary sector (services). Undeveloped economies typically start off as sustenance-based economies dependent on agriculture and natural resources. These economies then begin to manufacture goods when investment capital, research and development (R&D), and national infrastructure are aligned, and then finally progress to an economy based on services. Service-based economies are typically richer and have a higher quality of life than those based on agriculture and manufacturing.

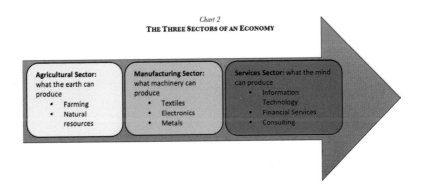

Chart 2
THE THREE SECTORS OF AN ECONOMY

Agricultural Sector: what the earth can produce
- Farming
- Natural resources

Manufacturing Sector: what machinery can produce
- Textiles
- Electronics
- Metals

Services Sector: what the mind can produce
- Information Technology
- Financial Services
- Consulting

When Deng took the helm in 1978, a large chunk of the economy (roughly one-third) was based on agricultural production, while services composed just one-fourth of economic output—both of which are signs that an economy is underdeveloped and needs modernization. Deng's modernizations are readily seen today, as just 15 percent of the economy is agricultural based, and services have more than doubled to 40 percent—almost at parity with manufacturing. By comparison, agriculture is responsible for just 1 percent of the United States' economic output, while services comprise 76 percent.[6] China has several more decades of modernization before its numbers look similar to these US figures and those of other Western nations.[7]

Had a leader like Deng not succeeded Mao, the dominos of goodwill between the two nations might not have fallen in order and would have likely resulted in continued economic stagnation. Deng's détente with the United States was the impetus behind several important events, such as the United States' 1978 decision to suspend formal diplomatic ties with Taiwan and its championing of Chinese WTO membership in the '90s. President Clinton normalized trade relations with China via the US-China Relations

Chart 3
PRE-DENG CHINESE GDP BY SECTOR, 1978

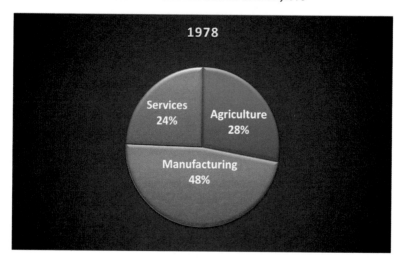

Chart 4
CHINESE GDP BY SECTOR, 2015

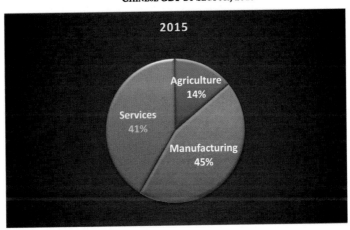

Note: Although less than 15 percent of China's 2015 GDP comes from agriculture, roughly 30 percent of all workers are still farmers, a disparity owing to the fact that the average Chinese farmer does not make much money and therefore contributes little GDP to the nation's total.

Act of 2000—legislation that lowered tariffs between the two and paved the way for WTO membership.

In light of many of the nefarious practices in which China has been engaging (currency manipulation, high tariffs, lack of worker protections, and lack of intellectual property protection), there is a sense that the United States "fast tracked" China's WTO bid in the 1990s without first ensuring that it satisfied many important requirements. The large business potential that many US corporations saw with China may have been a contributing factor to admitting China before it was ostensibly ready. Prior to attaining WTO membership, nations must demonstrate that they have low barriers to entry for imports (low tariffs), liberal and open trade policies, transparency, and a vibrant private economy based on free markets without government interference.[8] In the 1990s, the United States was able to use the threat of non-admittance as a trump card at US-Sino negotiations in order to push China to liberalize its economic policy and reduce state involvement in the private sector—a trump card that the United States can no longer play.

31

The next chapter will chronicle China's rise to become the world's second-largest economy, as its newly open market allows the nation of 1.38 billion citizens to engage in commerce across the globe.

Chapter 4

CHINA'S RISE TO NUMBER TWO

China's forty-year process of liberalizing its economy and opening up to international trade culminated in it passing Japan in GDP to become the world's second-largest economy in 2010. This rate of growth is nothing less than extraordinary, something not seen since America's great modernization during the late 1800s/early 1900s. To grasp the sheer scale and rapidity of this expansion, let's examine the size of China's GDP over the past twenty-five years:

1990: China's economy was the eleventh largest in the world, roughly one-fifth the size of Germany's and fifteen times smaller than the United States'. At this point, California's economy was larger than China's.

2000: China's economy became the sixth largest in the world.

2005: China surpassed France to become the fifth-largest economy and was now six times smaller than the United States'.

2010: From 2006 to 2010, China leapfrogged England, Germany, and finally, Japan. At this point, its economy was almost half the size of America's.

2016: By now, China is firmly entrenched as the second-largest economy, roughly two-thirds the size of America's. Its output is over twice the size of Japan's—only fifteen years prior, Japan's was four times the size of China's.[1]

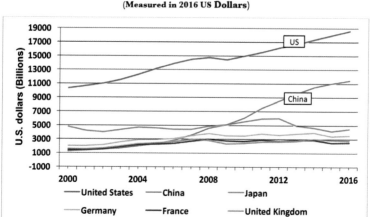

Chart 5
SELECT NATIONS' GROSS DOMESTIC PRODUCT (GDP), 2000–2016
(Measured in 2016 US Dollars)

This pace of growth is extraordinary and can be somewhat hard to comprehend; trends in economic output are typically small fluctuations—ebbs and flows—over time. There is generally some semblance of homeostasis or normalcy. For example, over any five-year stretch, economic output in France vis-à-vis Britain might flip flop, as it has several times over the past few decades, but in the end, the two countries typically end up at rough parity with each other.[2] Yet China is unique among nations and will likely continue its upward economic trajectory for four primary reasons:

1. It is still a developing nation.
2. Large segments of its population are still extremely poor.
3. The Communist Party is a strong and effective national body that can allocate and direct the entirety of the country's national resources at will.
4. Its population is enormous.

1. It is still a developing nation.

As a developing nation, the party bosses in China have many foci, but one in particular reigns supreme and can be summed up in three words: build, build, build. As the Chinese nation builds roads, railways, cities, amusement parks, telecommunications and fiber optics, hotels and houses, its GDP grows. As an example, let's list how many different industries and workers either are put to work or are involved in an ancillary capacity simply when a home is built:

- Lumber yards
- Concrete pourers
- Plumbers
- Masons
- Landscapers
- Foremen
- Window makers
- Architects
- Carpentry companies
- Durable goods producers (refrigerators/stoves/toilets)
- Real estate developers
- Real estate agents
- Home improvement stores
- Loan originators
- Appraisers
- Home security companies
- Banks (which provide home loans to consumers)
- The government (which provides loans to the banks)

This list is just for a single home. Now imagine when millions of these are built in conjunction with entire cities, highways, railways, and other infrastructure projects. Only then can you comprehend how China was able to maintain a growth rate of 10 percent or higher, year after year, decade after decade. The positive economic tailwinds of construction are prime reasons the government is intent on building as a matter of policy; it sometimes seems to be "building simply for the sake of building," as its ghost cities and non-performing construction projects can unfortunately attest to. The only downside to this is the painful realization that it is a one-shot deal: once a country has modernized and made that transformation, growth rates inevitably soften, as a nation does not just go around rebuilding skyscrapers and roads every couple of years. China has acknowledged this—its growth rate targets have dropped in recent years (currently hovering around 7 percent) and will likely drop to 6 percent within the next decade.[3] Once full modernization occurs, it will likely settle to the 3 to 5 percent level, as other Western nations have done once fully making the transition.

2.) Large segments of its population are still extremely poor.

Per capita GDP in the country is still low (roughly $8,000 a year), which means it has much room to grow.[4] As China's nascent middle class mushrooms, so does its GDP. When a Chinese peasant migrates to one of the coastal cities for work, this peasant might make twenty or thirty times more than when he/she worked on the farm. A peasant farmer works primarily for sustenance and doesn't have much money available for discretionary spending. Yet once in the middle class, this worker is now able to buy a range of goods previously unattainable, such as refrigerators, washers and dryers, a car, and maybe even a house—all of which increase GDP. In Western nations that already have a large and established middle class, wage increases (and, by proxy, GDP growth rates) are tempered. A US worker might get a 25 percent raise, and with this increase in income, he/she might buy new clothes or a bigger TV, but in reality, this worker's life will not change much, nor has this worker added much to the national economic output. That is why the modern economies of Japan, Europe, and the United States are currently expanding by between 1 to 3 percent, while poor nations in Africa and Asia can grow many multiples of that. Ethiopia grew at 8.7 percent in 2015, yet the powerful German economy expanded by just 1.5 percent.[5] However, the growth curve inevitably flattens as more and more citizens are lifted out of poverty, which results in fewer poor people left to make that large transition. China's trump card is that it is not even close to reaching this tipping point, as the nation still has roughly 450 million farmers and 200 million living in poverty.[6] America and the West went through this process of modernization and industrialization over a century ago, and China is going through it now. The only difference between America's nineteenth-century industrialization and China's is one of scale. In 1900, America's population was 76 million compared to China's 1.38 billion today, making China's growth potential exponentially greater.[7]

3.) The Communist Party is a strong and effective national body that can allocate and direct the entirety of the country's national resources at will.

For all of its human rights failings, China's Communist government has proven adept at prioritizing, resourcing, and implementing policies it deems to be of national importance. Ever since the Communists took over the mainland in 1949 following their civil war, the politburo has released five-year economic plans (most recently in 2016) in which it outlines, in concrete terms, its goals for the coming half decade. The unity of effort in prioritizing national issues is much of the reason China has consistently grown faster than its democratic Asian neighbor to the west (India), also an economic behemoth in waiting. As a developing nation with 1.32 billion and a per capita GDP of less than $2,000, India is often viewed as the "next China."[8] Yet in fledgling democracies like India's, establishing a common national theme or priority can be tough—every few years, there are elections, and newly elected leaders often augment or entirely roll back the policies of the prior administration. This issue is inherent in democratic systems and can be readily observed in Western nations like the United States, but it is more apparent and has deeper second- and third-order effects in new democracies that are still carving distinctive national identities.

Democratic governments have to cater to public opinion and temper their political ambitions to suit the public's wishes, even regarding policies that would be economically beneficial to the country. For example, it was generally accepted that the proposed Keystone XL Pipeline—designed to transport Canadian tar sands to

Texas for refinement and production—would be an economic boon to both the Canadian and American economies, as it would provide jobs, increase trade between two allies, and maintain stability in domestic oil markets. Oil production stability and availability is of prime importance because of the tenuous political relationship the United States has with many oil exporters. OPEC has, on several occasions, stopped producing oil as a result of political disagreements with the West—as was observed in the 1979 oil embargo. With all these benefits to the American economy, one would think that passing legislation to build Keystone XL would be a slam-dunk, yet it has been nothing of the sort. Since said legislation requires the participation of seven states to get the oil from Canada to Texas, it has to satisfy seven states worth of voters, seven states worth of towns with concerns about possible ecological impact, and dozens of Congressmen and women who might be opposed for political or moral reasons.[9] Therefore, it was debated and stalled for the better part of a decade and ultimately killed in 2016.

Contrast this to the Chinese government, where national priorities are set from the top and are adhered to like gospel. The Keystone XL Pipeline would have been built irrespective of public opinion to the contrary. Another example is the United States' efforts to rebuild the World Trade Center. While it took the United States a full thirteen years to overcome bureaucratic infighting and rebuild just a few buildings in downtown Manhattan, entire Chinese cities with hundreds of skyscrapers were constructed—seemingly overnight. This is why strong central governments with single-party rule can grow much quicker than democracies. Yet this advantage tends to be the case only in a nation's infancy, when government-led, large-scale national infrastructure projects are a necessity. Once all of the roads, cities, bridges, dams, power plants, and telecommunications are set up, the need for a dictatorial-based government to supplant private enterprise is lessened. What is needed then is a dynamic, fluid, entrepreneurial, and free enterprise–based economy. Remember, Microsoft was developed in a garage by a college dropout, not by a multibillion-dollar government-directed program. So while China may grow faster than India in the short term, India could prove more dynamic in the long run because of its less-centralized economic system.

4.) Its population is enormous.

Having 1.38 billion citizens can be challenging, especially for a ruling Communist Party constantly fearful of being overthrown via a popular uprising. Having to track, appease, and control that many people is not an easy undertaking, yet through its police-state style of control, the party has successfully been in power for almost seventy years unbroken. The benefits of having a population this size are undeniable, with the biggest benefit being quite obvious: potential for growth. Each of the 200 million peasant farmers who live off a dollar a day is potentially a future middle-class worker who could make large contributions to the economy. China's population advantage is immense—the average worker could still be considered "lower class" by Western standards, yet taken in totality, its citizenry might compose a sizable chunk of global GDP. Even with that per capita GDP of about $8,000, China is still the world's second-largest economy, which is what happens when you have seventeen times more people than Germany, nine times more people than Russia, and four times more people than the United States.[10]

Limited population size is part of the reason the industrious and sophisticated economies of Germany and Japan were never able reach parity with the United States in total economic size. Germany enjoyed a post–World War II economic boom and ironically came out of the war much stronger than its European peers that "won" the war. Gemany's *Wirtschaftwunder* (economic miracle) ushered in an era in which it had low inflation, rapid industrialization, superb education, and held the global technological high ground. This economic miracle propelled it past France and Great Britain to become the world's third-largest economy by the 1960s, and it comprised an impressive 9 percent of global output by 1969, less than three decades after it was completely ravaged by war.[11]

Japan's postwar miracle commenced later but was just as impressive. Its economy accounted for a whopping 17.8 percent of global output by the early 1990s, before its stock market and real estate crashes manifested in earnest—a correction so pervasive it is still recovering from it. To appreciate Japan's economic expansion from the 1970s to the early '90s, just consider this: In 1994, per

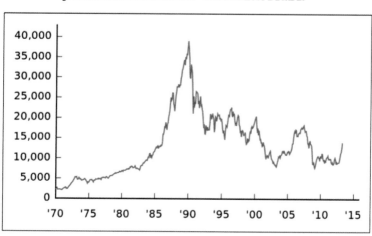

Chart 6
JAPANESE NIKKEI STOCK INDEX: "THE TWO LOST DECADES"

capita GDP in Japan was $38,000, compared to $28,000 for the average American, meaning that had populations been equal, Japan would have had an economy one-third larger than the United States'.[12] Had the respective populations of Germany and Japan been larger, both of these nations would have been able to make a more profound "splash" globally and reap the geopolitical benefits associated with greater economic clout. China does not have that demographic issue.[13]

Chapter 4 has been devoted to chronicling China's rise in becoming the world's second-largest economy, which by all accounts has been an extraordinary achievement. It is now clearly evident that by most metrics (economic health, military might, and future growth), China is firmly entrenched as the number two player globally. How far does it have to go in order catch up to the United States, the world's sole hyperpower? This next chapter will show how much China will have to climb in order to reach parity with the United States in military might, economic dominance, and geopolitical preeminence.

THE BENIGN HEGEMON

Contemporary international power dynamics are at a unique moment a decade and a half into the twenty-first century. Since the fall of the USSR in 1991, the United States has become the strongest country, relative to its peers, since the creation of the nation-state. Throughout civilized history, the hegemon at any given time has had viable counterweights—economically, militarily, or politically. In 1999, France's foreign minister Hubert Vedrine famously stated in the New York Times that he no longer defined the United States as a superpower but rather as a "hyperpower"—a newly coined term that best describes a country that was once a dominant figure in a bipolar world (United States and the former USSR during the Cold War) but is now predominant and preeminent in all categories.[1] The United States currently has no near peer, and in many areas, it is more prudent to compare it to the rest of the world instead of to any other nation or grouping of nations. Keep in mind that this dominance is held by a nation that encompasses only 4.4 percent of global population.[2]

1.) The United States has by far the most valuable and successful companies.

Of the five hundred biggest companies by stock market capitalization (the sum of all outstanding stock that gauges a company's worth), the United States garners fourteen out of the top fifteen slots, the lone foreign company being China's state-controlled China Mobile. With more than two hundred businesses making an appearance, American enterprises make up over 40 percent of the total list. China and the United Kingdom are next, at 7 and 6 percent, respectively.[3] As the most sought-after market for international investors, the US stock market is worth almost double that of the combined totals of Canada, China, France, Germany, Japan, Switzerland, and the United Kingdom.[4]

Chart 7
WORLD'S 15 LARGEST COMPANIES, 2016

Company	Market Cap (in Billions of USD)	Country
Apple	$522	US
Google	$483	US
Microsoft	$394	US
Exxon Mobil	$376	US
Berkshire Hathaway	$347	US
Amazon	$333	US
Facebook	$323	US
Johnson & Johnson	$317	US
General Electric	$281	US
AT&T	$250	US
Wells Fargo	$236	US
JPMorgan Chase	$227	US
China Mobile	$225	China
Proctor and Gamble	$221	US
Wal-Mart	$221	US

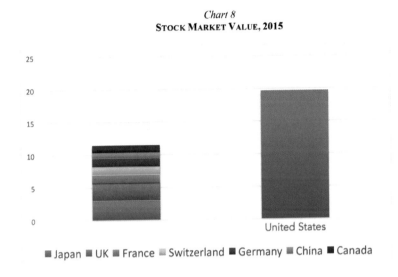

Chart 8
STOCK MARKET VALUE, 2015

■ Japan ■ UK ■ France ■ Switzerland ■ Germany ■ China ■ Canada

2.) The United States is the dominant player in higher education and research and development (R&D).

Times Higher Education publishes an annual list of the top universities across the globe, based on research excellence, knowledge transfer, resources, and business links. Of these universities, twenty-six of the top fifty are American, with the United Kingdom coming in second, with seven. US universities are a magnet for the world's aspiring youth, as there are over 1.13 million foreign-born students currently studying here. Chinese students are the largest cohort, with over 300,000. India, South Korea, Japan, and Saudi Arabia round off the list, each of which send their best and brightest—many of whom end up staying to work and live.[5]

Chart 9
TOP FIFTY UNIVERSITIES, 2015

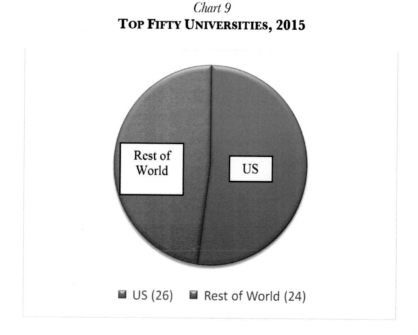

US (26) Rest of World (24)

3.) The US dollar is the only game in town when it comes to international transactions.

If a Guatemalan company wants to sell bananas to the Czech Republic, it does not trade in the Czech krona or the Guatemalan quetzal. Rather, it uses the US dollar. In fact, almost half of all international transactions have US dollars exchanging hands, as no other currency is as trusted or holds a stature comparable to that of the greenback.[6] The international community's reverence for the dollar affords the United States several unique advantages, such as low interests rates and political bargaining power, and makes it in the world's interest to keep the US economy and the dollar strong.[7]

Faith in the US dollar is beyond reproach, as it has been the international reserve currency of choice for decades. Nations buy reserves in other countries' currencies in order to manage

Chart 10
INTERNATIONAL TRANSACTIONS BY CURRENCY, 2012

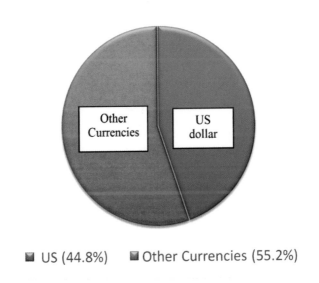

■ US (44.8%)   ■ Other Currencies (55.2%)

Chart 11
WORLD CURRENCY RESERVES BY TYPE, 2015

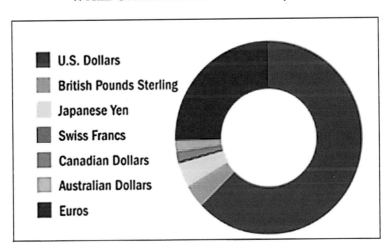

exchange rates and to offer stability to their financial systems during times of economic duress. When economic uncertainty exists, a nation needs stability and assets that will hold their value—and the dollar is the typical choice. In 2015, the US dollar made up 61 percent of global currency reserves (totaling $4 trillion), with the euro garnering 24 percent and no other currency reaching even 5 percent.[8]

4.) Its military might is unchallenged.

The United States' dominance in the national defense realm is often cited as one the most impressive concentrations of military might throughout history. The United States accounted for 37 percent of worldwide military spending in 2015—larger than the next seven countries combined.[9]

The size of its defense budget tells only part of the story, as it controls an extensive overseas military apparatus consisting of over eight hundred sprawling military bases spanning seventy countries with more than 200,000 troops deployed outside its

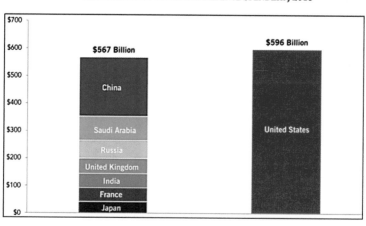

Chart 12
EIGHT LARGEST NATIONAL DEFENSE SPENDERS, 2015

borders at any given time.[10] The United States alone operates 95 percent of the world's overseas military bases, a system of foreign garrisons so enormous (1,300 square miles) that its total landmass is larger than the combined areas of Singapore, Bahrain, and Hong Kong. If its domestic base structure is included, the Department of Defense controls a swath of land larger than South Korea.[11] No other nation is able to station even one-tenth the numbers of troops the United States does internationally. Even the British were struggling to maintain 15,000 troops in Iraq/Afghanistan, while the Americans had an enduring deployed force of over 150,000 for almost a decade.[12] It is the only nation that has the ability to project power in every corner of the globe, with over 40,000 troops each in Germany and Japan, 25,000 troops in South Korea, over 10,000 in Italy and Kuwait, and thousands more scattered in smaller confines.

With the backing of 5,000 aircraft, many of which are technological marvels with a sticker price of over $250 million apiece, the US Air Force is the preeminent aerial power on the planet, roughly one-third larger than the world's next most powerful air force: the US Navy/US Marine Corps. The US Navy and Marine Corps boast 3,400 airframes, capable of deploying anywhere in the world via ship. Put together, the US Air Force, Navy, and Marine Corps have more aircraft and firepower than the next ten nations combined.[13]

Naval force is often cited as the preferred way to project power internationally, as these large fleets are essentially floating bases with awesome military capabilities. The US Navy currently deploys eleven aircraft carrier strike groups (no other nation has more than one), each of which is able to carry over sixty fighter and bomber aircraft. The US Navy can carry twice as many aircraft at sea as the rest of the world combined, and under the sea, the United States has fifty-seven nuclear-powered attack and cruise-missile submarines—also more than the rest of the world combined.[14] Naval power and its system of overseas land bases affords the United States vast leverage in security, economic, and political discussions.

5.) It wins far more Nobel Prizes than any other nation.

Since 1901, Nobel Prizes have been awarded for outstanding achievements in physics, chemistry, literature, medicine, and peace. It is widely regarded as one of the major forums where the brightest and most innovative minds are honored for their achievements. Nobel Prizes (particularly in the sciences) offer insight into a nation's entrepreneurial capacity and ability to develop new ideas and theories. Again, the United States dominates here, as it receives 40 percent of all Nobel Prizes and is especially dominant in physiology and medicine. Owing to their world-class research centers and universities, the UK and Germany are awarded next most often, yet even their combined totals pale in comparison to the US.[15]

THESE STATISTICS MAY COME as a surprise to many Americans, as domestic political pundits from the non-ruling party tend to paint an image of America in disarray, in decline, and besieged by rising foreign powers. As these figures show, in areas ranging from university education to the financial dynamism of American companies, military might, Nobel Prizes for outstanding achievements, and faith in US currency, there is no peer nor any other nation even in the same conversation. America's dominance is unique and seems to fly under the radar because it was the only global hegemon throughout civilized history that has not used its might for imperial ambitions or world conquest. For example, the defeated nations of Germany and Japan were not absorbed as additional US states; rather, they were nursed back to economic health via United States–led reconstruction efforts such as the Marshall Plan. Their nations were also sheltered under the umbrella of the US military, which kept hundreds of thousands of troops there in order to provide stability. The fact that the United States didn't absorb a single acre of foreign territory from the spoils of World War II (in contrast to the Russians), nor during the seventy years that followed, is the reason it has been deemed the "benign hegemon." Its perceived benignity stems from a leadership style that stresses four key pillars:

1. The United States has used its power to establish a set of open global institutions that have been broadly beneficial writ large:

   UN
   WTO
   IMF
   World Bank
   GATT (General Agreement on Tariffs and Trade)
   ILO (International Labor Organization)
   OECD (Organization for Economic Cooperation and Development)

2. The United States, for the most part, has led the world through inclusion and consent rather than coercion.

3. When the United States has used military force, it has largely done so to uphold human rights and international peace, security, and prosperity. It has also used force only when there was broad international consensus.

4. The United States has, for the most part, used its power to promote democracy, human rights, and rule of law.

Note: Although the United States has for the most part kept its end of the bargain with respect to numbers 3 and 4, there are notable exceptions that exist—which its opponents have used to undermine its tacit rule: the United States' military adventurism during the 2003 invasion of Iraq was executed preemptively, without direct military provocation and without UN Security Council approval. The CIA's overthrow of democratically elected Iranian prime minister Mohammad Mossadegh in 1953 (installing the shah in the process) flies in the face of its supposed blanket support for democracy. It also has a history of supporting autocratic regimes, notably in the Arab world, so long as they are sympathetic to US interests.

Chapter 5 laid out the United States' economic/military dominance and geopolitical reach—a set of dynamics that should have inertia and staying power well into the twenty-first century. Chapter 6 will discuss the underpinnings of US-Sino economic links and why it will provide for a stable bilateral relationship in the future.

Chapter 6

INDISPENSABLE PARTNERS

It is no secret that trade and economic interconnectedness are the foremost links that keeps this relationship afloat. Fortunately for both sides, money and the likelihood of future prosperity are powerful motivators for keeping this arrangement stable, for these are two nations that have little else in common. China has a rich history encompassing more than four thousand years of unimpeded civilization, while the United States is an infant by comparison, as the first British colony was established there in the early 1600s. The United States and China also differ in cultural aspects, as Chinese ethos are guided by the principles of Confucianism, which focuses on social harmony, order, and human/familial relationships. While social cohesion is one tenet of Confucian thought, the United States espouses the primacy of the individual and self-reliance over all—which is why it is also fervently capitalist and has never had a strong penchant for socialist policies. The five relationships that govern Confucian order are:

1. Father to son
2. Elder brother to younger brother
3. Husband to wife
4. Ruler to subject
5. Friend to friend

Chart 13
US-SINO CULTURAL AND HISTORICAL DIFFERENCES

	China	United States
Civilized History	4,000+ years	400 years
Guiding Principles on Morality	Confucianism	Judeo-Christian teachings
Social Priority	The society	The individual
Government System	Single-party rule (Communist party)	Representative Democracy
Regional Adversaries in Asia	Japan, Taiwan	North Korea

These are also ethnically differing nations, as the United States is a patchwork of various backgrounds, religions, and ethnicities, while over 91 percent of China is from a single ethnicity (Han Chinese).[1] While the United States is a nation of immigrants, China has no history of large-scale immigration to the mainland. There are also deep historical, military, and political "third rail" issues between the nations, such as disagreements over the South/East China Seas and foreign relations policies with Japan, Taiwan, and North Korea. These geopolitical divergences cause profound divides and mutual distrust that will be discussed in chapter 7.

By all accounts, these two behemoths should not have a deep and stable relationship, yet as mentioned before, the primary link binding them is a powerful one: money. In 2015, bilateral trade totaled $598 billion—a larger figure than the entire economic output of all but twenty countries on the planet.[2] US-Sino trade has more than doubled in the past decade and has grown an amazing twenty-four-fold in the past twenty-five years.[3]

Globalization is the prime mover behind this increase in trade, as goods can be produced and shipped internationally in a more efficient manner than at any previous time. The "levelling of the playing field" allows countries with lower-paid workers (such as

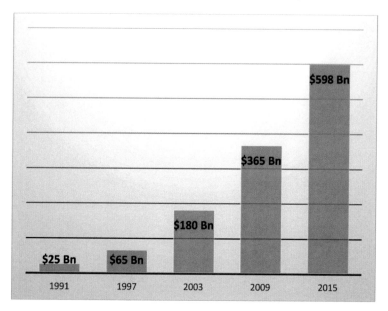

Chart 14
US/CHINA BILATERAL TRADE, 1991–2015
(non-inflation adjusted US dollars)

China) to sell their goods on the open market cheaper than nations whose citizens warrant higher compensation. However, there are many competing viewpoints and arguments on whether the influx of trade over the past few decades has been mutually beneficial or whether it is a zero-sum game, whereby gains by one nation correspond with comparable losses in another.

It is my belief that trade is symbiotically beneficial for both of these nations, but for very different reasons. The phrase "the consumer is king" is characteristic of the US economy, as over two-thirds of GDP is based on the consumption of goods and services.[4] In capitalist and free market–based economies, the consumer wins when he/she can buy the best products for the cheapest price, irrespective of which country produced them. Although the United States has experienced massive industrial job losses—millions of manufacturing jobs have been shipped overseas, to China in particular—it must be understood that the shifting makeup of certain industries is a natural function of the capitalist system, which benefits world markets, as well as the US economy, in the long run.

Let's use the example of the village blacksmith to illustrate this viewpoint. The production and sale of automobiles in the early twentieth century clearly put the village blacksmith in a bind. He could either push for protectionism against the introduction of automobiles (high taxes on cars, bureaucratic red tape, and other barriers to entry) in an effort to save his industry for the short term or he could see the writing on the wall and pick up a new skill in order to be a part of this revolutionary invention. For better or worse, the blacksmith needed to understand that the need for his unique skill in making horseshoes was becoming obsolete, and the automobile allowed for a more efficient (and eventually cheaper) traveling experience for the consumer. He should therefore not stand in the way of progress. Although the blacksmith may have suffered short-term pain, it was better for the consumer and the country as a whole to have automobiles instead of horse-drawn buggies.

The contemporary US manufacturing sector draws many parallels to this example; it is foolish to try to artificially protect industries suffering at the hands of globalization and technological advancement. Yes, these industries may be spared in the interim, but the move would end up harming the consumer and the nation at large, solely to save jobs that are heading toward extinction. These industries should be viewed as the modern-day blacksmith. The blacksmith example illustrates one of the basic tenants of capitalism, a tenant that has allowed the consumer to purchase higher-quality products for ever-decreasing prices for several centuries. If there is one chart in this book that needs to be tabbed and referenced whenever there is a discussion on long-term trends of the US economy, it would be Chart 15. It is important to take notice of the following facts:

- Agriculture has been the smallest sector of our economy for well over one hundred years and has been in decline since the Industrial Revolution.
- Manufacturing last reached parity with services in the early 1900s and has been in regular decline since the 1950s.

Chart 15
US GDP BY SECTOR, 1840–2010

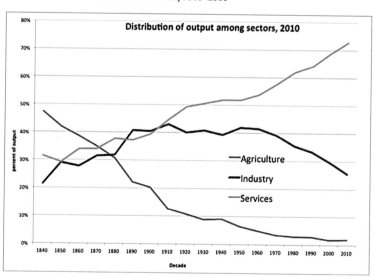

- Services compose over 75 percent of our economy and have been the majority sector since the 1930s.[5]

As mentioned in chapter 3, the sectoral progression from agriculture to manufacturing and, finally, to services is the natural process an economy takes when it undergoes modernization. Those who deride globalization and outsourcing, claiming they are responsible for the decline in US manufacturing, are missing the point. Manufacturing decline in favor of services *should* be a nation's goal, as affluence is typically coupled with the service sector. Consider this: Facebook (a 12-year-old company that doesn't make anything) is now worth more than General Electric (a 130-year-old industrial giant founded by Thomas Edison that makes everything from wind turbines to jet engines). This example demonstrates the power and exponential earning potential of the "information age" over the "industrial age."

Manufacturing decline is not a new phenomenon; US manufacturing has been in decline for seven decades, during a time when the United States has enjoyed vast wealth and standard of living increases. Those who long for the United States' "golden age" of manufacturing are

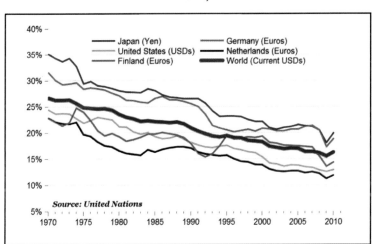

Chart 16
SELECT WESTERN NATIONS' MANUFACTURING SECTOR AS A
PERCENTAGE OF GDP, 1970–2010

longing for a time that likely hasn't existed since well before they were born. Even in the 1950s and '60s (commonly cited as the prime years of US manufacturing), services contributed roughly one-third more to the economy than manufacturing. One would have to go back to the 1910s to observe the last time manufacturing outstripped services.[6] Chart 16 shows that progression away from manufacturing toward services has been a common trend among Western nations since the 1970s (even in industrial powerhouses like Germany and Japan). This is a trend that China will eventually experience as its economy modernizes—once it has a solid middle class that demands higher wages, industry will be moved abroad to lower-cost nations still in their developmental stage.[7]

The producer-consumer relationship between the United States and Chinese workers has increased the quality of life for both sides. For China, it has brought tens of millions of farmers to the coast to find higher-paying jobs, and for America, it has ushered in an era of unprecedented purchasing power. Let's look at a real-world example to illustrate the point about how the influx of low-cost products not only helps the Chinese but is also a boon to American consumers. If US consumers had $5,000 to purchase goods in 1995

Chart 17
**GLOBALIZATION AND ITS EFFECT ON THE AFFORDABILITY OF
GOODS FOR THE AMERICAN CONSUMER**

US Consumer's Purchasing Power in 1995		US Consumer's Purchasing Power in 2016	
Desktop PC	$3,400	65-inch flat screen TV	$1,250
36-inch TV	$1,400	Couch set	$750
20 VHS movies	$200	Smart phone	$400
		Surround sound speakers	$400
		Smart watch	$250
		Laptop	$250
		Desktop PC	$200
		Netflix for 1 yr	$120
		Leftover cash	$1,380

(prior to China's admittance to the WTO) versus 2015, how much more bang for their buck would they get? The consumers in 1995 would not get much more than a Pentium-90 computer complete with a 540mb hard drive, a thirty-six-inch RCA television set, and twenty or so VHS cassettes.[8] They would also have to go to the store, stand in line, physically buy this merchandise, and haul it home. Conversely, in 2015, they would be able to buy a sixty-five-inch flat-screen TV, a laptop computer, a desktop computer, a smartphone, a smart watch (which by itself has more computing power than the 1995 Pentium-90), Netflix for an entire year, five-speaker surround sound, and a three-piece couch set to lounge on while enjoying these products. Furthermore, all these products can be bought online, shipped for free via Amazon.com, and delivered in two or three days.[9] Did I mention that even after all of those purchases, the 2015 consumer would still have almost $1,400 left?[10]

Granted, much of the consumer's increase in purchasing power is due to technological advances, but a significant component is the fact that these goods can be produced en masse by inexpensive foreign labor and shipped stateside. In 1995, Chinese imports to America made up a paltry $50 billion; by 2016, that figure had risen eight-fold, to $400 billion. It is not a coincidence that over the past three decades, as US consumers enjoyed the benefits of ever-decreasing prices, cross-border trade has increased 560 percent, while trade as a percentage of GDP jumped from 13 percent in 1987 to over 20 percent today.[11] China's free market reforms have brought 680 million people out of poverty since 1980, largely as a result of its ability to trade with the United States and the West. Amazingly, three out of every four people globally who have been lifted out of poverty during this timeframe were Chinese.[12]

Now that we have discussed why this relationship between the consumers (United States) and producers (China) is a solid fit for both sides, let's look into how this trade dynamic has continued its upward trajectory unabated for the past few decades. In order for

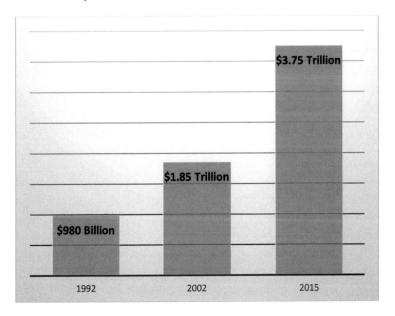

Chart 18
TOTAL US TRADE, 1992–2015
(NON-INFLATION-ADJUSTED US DOLLARS)

$3.75 Trillion

$1.85 Trillion

$980 Billion

1992   2002   2015

China to sell its products, it needs buyers who have money and will continue their purchasing habits well into the future. Luckily for China, the US consumer exists—a legion of buyers who constitute less than 5 percent of the world's population yet consume over 25 percent of its goods. One would need to combine the next five countries (China, Japan, Germany, United Kingdom, and France) to equal the power of the US consumer market.[13] China linked its national currency, the yuan (often referred to as the renminbi), to the US dollar starting in 1994. It did this for several reasons. First, since the United States was the largest economy and largest consuming class by far, Chinese exporters could "target" it better by maintaining stability with fixed exchange rates that would give it known cost/profit margins. Second, linking the yuan to the dollar protected the yuan against currency fluctuations, which can wreak havoc for exporters. Free-floating currencies can oscillate several percentage points weekly and are a slave to the law of supply and demand, as well as macroeconomic happenings beyond a nation's control. If an exporting nation's currency (like the Chinese yuan) suddenly rises in value against a currency it does a large amount of business with (like the US dollar), its products become more expensive and less attractive essentially overnight, causing slower growth and even economic contraction. While this concept is a necessary evil for most countries, fluctuation in growth rates is not something the party bosses at the Chinese politburo can risk.

The Communist Party's priority is to stay in power and usher in a prosperous and stable China in the twenty-first century. Because modern China was born out of a revolution (an occurrence leaders are vying to prevent from happening again), the government has resorted to several extreme methods in order to maintain stability. These include a robust propaganda apparatus, a closely monitored internet, limits on civil society and individual freedoms, and (most importantly) a focus on regular and sustained economic growth. Conventional thinking among the politburo is that revolutionary sentiment and demand for civil liberties would be a low priority for the citizenry if the nation were prospering economically and people were becoming more affluent; this is why the yuan needs to be linked to the dollar. Although the yuan weaned itself off the dollar peg in

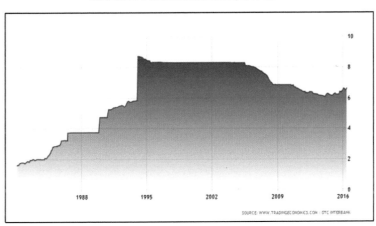

Chart 19
US DOLLAR-YUAN EXCHANGE RATE, 1985–2016

2005 after eleven years, Chart 19 shows that the yuan is still managed (albeit more loosely) to temper wild currency swings against the greenback. Also of note in Chart 19 is the instant weakening of the yuan in 1994 upon institution of the peg, resulting in a whopping eight-to-one exchange rate after being two-to-one just a decade earlier.

By linking its currency to the dollar, China is able to artificially lower its exchange rate in order to make its goods cheaper. On the surface, one wonders why a nation would want to weaken its currency until it is understood that China is still a relatively poor nation by Western standards. Its citizens don't consume much; only one-third of their GDP is based off consumption, they have a high savings rate, and their per capita GDP is only $8,000. With those dynamics in mind, a weak national currency that targets external consumers makes absolute sense.[14]

Moving forward, it's imperative to discuss US debt and China's purchasing of US treasury bonds, a subject of great consternation and anxiety among many Americans. Although an outsized debt-to-GDP ratio is a recipe for economic stagnation, the contemporary bilateral policy of buying/selling US treasuries (debt) is a symbiotic relationship that economically benefits both sides. Like most advanced nations, the US government has yearly budget deficits as it borrows and invests near-term with the idea of having those investments pay dividends in the future via increased economic growth. For most of the twentieth century and into the twenty-first, the United States has run yearly budget deficits as it paid for World War II, Vietnam, its military buildup in the '80s, the Bush-era wars in the Middle East, periodic tax cuts, and social programs such as Medicare/Medicaid. Save for a few years during Clinton's presidency, the United States has not had a budget surplus for close to five decades.[15] Deficit spending is not necessarily a bad thing, especially if it is funded domestically via a nation's citizenry buying government bonds—the norm for most of the twentieth century. Yet as Americans started to save less, consume more, and buy fewer bonds, the US government needed to commence selling bonds on the international market to make up the difference. Export-heavy and resource-rich nations that maintain yearly budget surpluses were all too happy to park their investment capital in US treasury bonds (T-Bonds), as US debt is regarded as safe and stable—the gold standard of bond investments. In the late 1990s/early 2000s, China started buying T-Bonds in earnest to keep the yuan artificially low and maintain its trade surplus with the United States. In 2000, China held only $68 billion in US bonds, a number that had increased twenty-fold to $1.3 trillion by 2016.[16] Large foreign holdings of US debt might seem undesirable at first, but they are one of the underlying reasons the United States currently pays under 2 percent on its ten-year notes, while it paid over 15 percent in the 1970s (Chart 20). This relationship allows the United States to save hundreds of billions of dollars in interest payments.

Those with a basic understanding of macroeconomics know that under normal market forces, a trade deficit will cause a nation's currency to fall because there is now an excess supply of that currency floating around (in this case, the US dollar). Conversely, the exporting nation's currency (the yuan) should rise in kind, therefore scoring this issue of supply/demand and greatly reducing the trade imbalance. One of the ways China is able to maintain such staggering trade surpluses with the United States is by creating artificial demand in the US dollar by buying large swaths of its debt (T-bonds), thereby propping up the dollar's value against the yuan.[17]

Chart 20
YIELD ON TEN-YEAR US TREASURY BONDS, 1960–2015

Source: Federal Reserve.

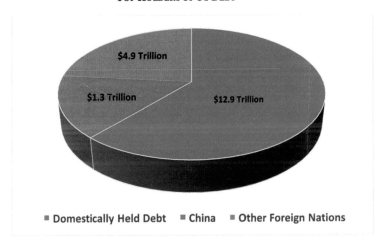

Chart. 21
TOP HOLDERS OF US DEBT

Although China's holdings of US debt are often viewed as a trump card that places it in a dominant position when it comes to US-Sino political negotiations, the truth is that it is in China's interests to buy US debt, and selling its T-bonds on the open market would harm its economy. If China were to dump its bonds or scale back its

61

yearly purchases, the dollar would weaken, and the yuan would rise drastically—greatly diminishing China's ability to sell to its biggest consumer. Since the average Chinese consumes a fraction of the average American, domestic consumption would not be able to pick up the slack left in the wake of the American consumer. Lack of exports would equate to slower GDP growth, which, as stated earlier, is the government's number one concern and the biggest risk in having its citizens revolt against its single-party system of authoritarian rule. Furthermore, if China tries to foment anxiety by threatening to sell its US debt, it would be akin to "cutting your nose to spite your face," as it would cause China to lose vast amounts of value in its investment. Since it owns $1.3 trillion of these bonds, it would be in China's interest to keep the dollar and its investment strong. If the dollar is worthless, so too would its bonds be worthless upon redemption. For this reason, the status quo will remain, for it serves both nations' interests—the Chinese can keep their currency weak and make their exports attractive, while the Americans can finance their debt cheaply and consume more via their stronger currency. It is for this reason that the US debt and the dollar-yuan relationship compose one of the primary tenants of this marriage.

After absorbing the data, figures, charts, and (some) opinions in this chapter, the reader can understand why this marriage is so robust. On one hand, there's America—a rich and developed nation

Chart 22

BILATERAL BENEFITS OF CHINA BUYING US DEBT

US	China
Raises value of the dollar and boosts purchasing power of US consumers	Keeps yuan weak which boosts exports
Can finance government debt cheaply	Supplies China with the world's most stable investment (US T-bonds)

that has progressed from the industrial age to the information age and must therefore buy much of its goods outside its borders. Its immense consuming class is the envy of the world's manufacturers, who salivate at the prospect of getting their products to American shores. On the other hand, there's China—a large and developing nation that is still agrarian/manufacturing based and has the infrastructure and national will in place to produce and sell goods en masse to overseas consumers. Of these markets, the United States is the most coveted, so the Chinese market their products primarily to the American consumer.

The ultimate manifestation of robust US-Sino relations would be the creation of a bilateral organization (tacitly referred to as the G-2) in which they are the sole members and decision makers—a reality that may be slowly coming to fruition. Economic and security matters of global importance are routinely held at summits of two multinational organizations: the G-7 and the G-20. The former consists of Canada, France, Germany, Italy, Japan, the United Kingdom, and the United States, while the latter includes the G-7 plus thirteen emerging market nations, led by China. With the rise of emerging markets, the G-20 has been gaining favor in recent years over the G-7 and is widely viewed as the more vital organization, especially with respect to economics. And within the G-20, there has been growing chatter of United States–China side meetings that have been deemed the G-2. At these G-2 meetings, the United States and China can talk more candidly and have more latitude for political discourse, the thought being that if they can agree on issues bilaterally, the rest of the G-20 would likely follow suit in support. In 2009, Foreign Affairs editor Fred Bergsten described the profound importance of the G-2:

> There will be no sustained recovery from the current global economic crisis unless the United States and China lead it. There will be no renewed momentum toward progress on global trade, unless they endorse it. There will be no international compact on global warming unless they embrace it. The United States and China are the world's two most important economies: the United States leads the high-income economies, and China leads

the emerging-market economies. The United States and China are the two largest trading countries and the two largest polluters. The United States is the world's largest deficit/debtor country, and China is the world's largest surplus/creditor country—and there will be no resolution of the global imbalances that helped bring on the current crisis, nor lasting reform of the international financial architecture, without their concurrence. Hence, an effective G-2 is imperative if the world economy is to move forward both cyclically and structurally. [18]

Chapter 7

STRATEGIC MISTRUST

While the past several chapters chronicled China's peaceful rise to number two, chapter 7 will focus on many of the historical, political, and military issues that could cause friction down the line, especially as China's capacity to challenge the United States increases. The major Sino-American points of contention discussed in this chapter are: 1) relations with Taiwan, North Korea, and Japan; 2) the South and East China Seas dispute; and 3) US-China trade issues.

Taiwan Relations

The single most important territorial issue facing China today is the fact that the island of Taiwan is not under its authority and operates as an autonomous and democratic pseudo-state. Although not considered a country under strict international law, it has its own national flag, Olympic team, passport, currency, government, president, and foreign relations. Twenty-two nations recognize Taiwan as an independent country, yet if it were to declare full independence and apply for reentry into the UN, China would declare war instantaneously. Therefore, for the near-term, there is a relative status quo both sides adhere to that provides relative stability. The status quo is as follows: there is but one China; the only issue is that both sides claim to be the sole shepherds of this title.

Imperial Japan ruled Taiwan following its victory in the Sino-Japanese War until its defeat in World War II fifty years later. From the mid-1920s until 1949, China fought a civil war between the Communist forces led by Mao Zedong and the Nationalists (KMT), both of whom were jockeying to become the legitimate successor of the dynastic rule that had led China for centuries. It was an intermittent struggle, as the Chinese temporarily coalesced as one nation in order to battle Japan's military incursions on their coastline during World War II and in Manchuria in the 1930s. Once hostilities with the Japanese ended, the civil war began again in earnest until the KMT Party retreated to Taiwan to set up its government, while the Communists claimed victory on the mainland. As of 1949, mainland China and Taiwan were now two separate entities and were referred to as the People's Republic of China (PRC) and Republic of China (ROC), respectively.

There was no armistice or peace treaty signed after hostilities ended, resulting in both sides claiming to be the sole and legitimate leader of all of China. Owing to its deep sense of pride in its position as the Middle Kingdom, the civilization can be considered whole again only once there is geographic unity; this is why China views Taiwan's independence with such vitriol. Compounding this issue is the lack of international clarity on the topic. The UN was established in 1945 (while the Chinese civil war was still being fought), with the five main World War II victors installed as the shepherds of international peace and security as members of the UN Security Council. These members were the United States, United Kingdom, France, Russia, and the ROC. Although the civil war was still being played out, the United States supported the Nationalist KMT government with money and military hardware, as it was fervently anti-communist—especially with the budding Cold War with the USSR. Once the Nationalists were driven to Taiwan and it was evident that the Communists had won the war, the UN still decided to recognize Taiwan (ROC) as the sole legal representative of all of China, even though it is only 14,000 square miles compared to China's 3.7 million, with a fraction of the mainland's population (9.8 million versus 500 million).[1] Taiwan kept this status until 1971, when the UN passed Resolution 2758, which stripped statehood from the ROC and switched recognition to the PRC, deeming it the lone and legitimate representative of China to the United Nations.[2] The vote was passed thirty-five to seventy-six, with the United States casting its support in favor of Taiwan keeping its seat.

In 1979, after a détente between China and the United States as a result of warming relations via high-level meetings—first between Nixon/Kissinger and Mao, then between President Carter and Deng Xiaoping—the United States switched recognition of the Chinese state from the government of Taipei (Taiwan) to the government of Beijing (China). This formerly ended its diplomatic recognition of Taiwan as an independent state. However, to reassure its support for the island's security after the vote, in 1979 the United States signed the Taiwan Relations Act, which

> provides the legal basis for the unofficial relationship between the United States and Taiwan, and enshrines the U.S. commitment to assist Taiwan in maintaining its defensive capability. The United States insists on the peaceful resolution of cross-strait differences, opposes unilateral changes to the status quo by either side, and encourages dialogue to help advance such an outcome.[3]

The United States' exporting of weapons to Taiwan is a major source of ire from China, as it views this action as an impediment to it reclaiming what it sees as a breakaway province that needs to be absorbed. The United States sold Taiwan $12 billion in military hardware from 2010 to 2015, producing frequent diplomatic protests from the mainland.[4]

Although the United States' links with China over the past few decades have become increasingly robust, it still obligates itself to ensure the survival of Taiwan. In response to the buildup of China-Taiwan tensions resulting in the "Third Taiwan Strait Crisis" of 1995–96, President Clinton responded sharply by sending two aircraft carrier battle groups to the region—even sailing one through the small strait that separates the two belligerents. This tremendous show of force coerced China to back down, as it was in no position to challenge the US military at the time. Yet if this same issue were to manifest itself in 2025 instead of 1995, would the United States have the same response, especially now that power dynamics have shifted? US policymakers will have to ask themselves whether supporting a tiny island of 23 million while drawing rage and potential military conflict from our largest importer and 1.38 billion people is a policy worth reconsidering. Anti-Communist ideological inertia from the Cold War could be driving our policy stance on Taiwan, and what might be needed is a comprehensive, pragmatically framed study into the contemporary cost-benefit dynamic of US-Taiwan relations as they are currently. Either way, the United States is in a delicate position: it needs to assure Taiwan and the world that America adheres to its diplomatic agreements without question (in this case, the 1979 Taiwan Relations Act), yet it also needs to not compound an already tense situation and get drawn into an unnecessary conflict with China.

North Korea Relations

The United States and China stand on opposite ends of the spectrum with respect to North Korea—a pariah state that operates outside international law and UN agreements. Its closed society and lack of trade and communication with the outside world has resulted in economic stagnation in the most extreme sense. Its 2015 GDP came in at a paltry $28 billion, or roughly $1,000 per capita.[5] To put in perspective how poor this nation is, consider that a single US company (Apple) is valued at over $500 billion, which equates to seventeen years of North Korea's total economic output. China is the central reason North Korea is able to exist, affording it military hardware and basic goods that ensure its survival. The United States and the West continually prod China behind closed doors to push the Jung Un regime to sanitize the rhetoric coming out of the country, as he continually threatens the peace and security in the region.

Although the unpredictable tyrant is a liability for the Chinese as well, North Korea provides a buffer between the mainland and the 28,000 US troops stationed on South Korean soil. Should North Korea dissolve as a state and be reunified under the South, China would then share an 880-mile-long border with a nation that has a mutual defense treaty with the United States—a situation the Chinese would never allow. Also, should the North fall, millions of refugees would pour over the border into southern China, which would cause civil unrest and stress the nation's social system. More than 150,000 Chinese were killed during the Korean War, primarily to support their communist brethren and ensure that the South Koreans and the Americans were repelled back down to the thirty-eighth parallel—a comfortable distance from the Chinese border.

Japan Relations

Relations with Japan are another issue that causes US-Sino friction, as many of China's recent military defeats came at the hands of Imperial Japan. The Chinese were the dominant player in the region for much of their more than four-thousand-year history and view Japan's string of military victories over the last century as a matter of national shame that must be avenged. The fact that Japan has not publicly acknowledged its war-crime atrocities against the Chinese and their prime ministers still make visits to World War II shrines are two sources of friction cited by the mainlanders. Japanese denouncements from the Chinese politburo have resulted in an intermittent increase in tensions, resulting in boycotts of Japanese goods and vandalism of Japanese stores on the mainland in recent years. As China's power is waxing and Japan's is waning (China finally surpassed Japan's GDP in 2010 after over a century of being the lesser economy), China is now more willing to confront the Japanese (and, by proxy, the United States).

US-Japan relations have provided stability in East Asia for many decades, guided by the 1960 American-Japanese security treaty that commits the United States to defend Japan if it were to come under attack. Japan also provides the United States with geostrategic depth, as it hosts over 40,000 US troops and the US Navy's 7th Fleet. As Japan revisits shedding its post–World War II pacifism and looks to remain a strong regional player in East Asia, it is looking at an expanded US military presence and closer cooperation as means to those ends. A 2015 revised military agreement between the two nations reassures Japan—which has many doubts about its ability to meet its security challenges in East Asia—particularly on how to cope with the surging military power and diplomatic confidence of China. The United States and Japan are in broad agreement about how best to manage a rising China, which gives credence to the Chinese mantra that the United States is unduly involving itself in their regional affairs.[6]

South and East China Seas Dispute

Over the past several years, eight nations (Brunei, China, Indonesia, Japan, Malaysia, Taiwan, Philippines, and Vietnam) have been disputing ownership of several island chains in the South and East China Seas. Most of these islands are uninhabitable and have not been a point of contention until recently, when several nations publicly claimed them as sovereign territory. The geographic importance of these islands are huge; 40 percent of global trade passes through these seas, meaning international trade can be controlled by whichever nation controls these specks of rock.[7] Also, with the possibility of oil and fishing rights around each of the islands' two-hundred-nautical-mile Exclusive Economic Zone (EEZ), there is an additional economic component at play. China has begun constructing man-made islands in the South China Sea—complete with runways and permanent structures (ostensibly for military means)—as a way to solidify its sphere of influence in the region. To compound this already complex issue, Chinese claims are based on their 1947 "nine dash line," which has not been internationally recognized. Map 1 shows China's nine dash line, as well as the claims by four other nations, while Map 2 shows claims by two more nations in the East China Sea (Taiwan/Japan). (Note:

Indonesia is not pictured in these maps, yet there have been several reports of Chinese-Indonesian territorial disputes in recent years.)[8]

In 2016, the Permanent Court of Arbitration at The Hague ruled that China had no legal basis for its claims—rulings that China vehemently stated it will not abide by. The United States routinely sends warships to the region to ensure allies like the Philippines, Japan, and Taiwan that it will play a role in ensuring this issue is resolved without Chinese coercion over its smaller neighbors. China has publicly denounced the United States' "freedom of maneuver" naval exercises in the region, proclaiming that it is meddling in regional affairs that do not concern it. As stated in chapter 1 and

Map 1

TERRITORIAL CLAIMS IN THE SOUTH CHINA SEA

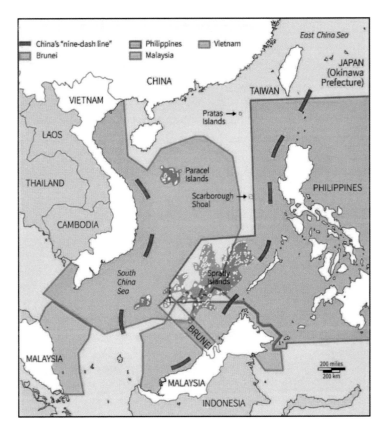

Map 2
TERRITORIAL CLAIMS IN THE EAST AND SOUTH CHINA SEA

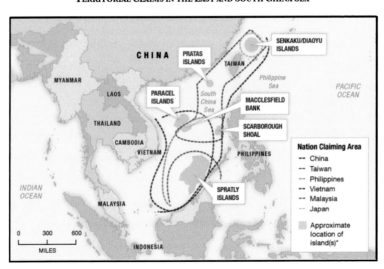

earlier in this chapter, China views a return to full territorial integrity (a return of Taiwan and control of the South/East China Seas) as paramount to righting the wrongs of the Century of Humiliation. As the United States continues to operate in the region and make the patrols more routine, China has increased the intensity of its military and political responses, announcing in its state-run newspaper:

> *In the face of the US harassment, Beijing should deal with Washington tactfully and prepare for the worst. We need to convince the White House that China, despite its unwillingness, is not frightened to fight a war with the US in the region, and is determined to safeguard its national interests and dignity. The United States has been very irresponsible and we will take any measures necessary to safeguard our security. I advise the US not to make a fool out of themselves in trying to be smart.*[9]

Aggressive rhetoric like this may simply be used to placate Communist Party hardliners, or it may be a harbinger of things to come as this issue continues without resolution.

US-China Trade Issues

The first few topics of this chapter centered on political, territorial, and historical issues, yet the final one is based strictly on economics and trade. Although the influx of trade should bring stability to the relationship, it also has the potential to stoke tensions, as shifting economic realities cause jobs and industries to be shifted and outsourced. The US economy may be harmed by the mounting evidence that China is not playing by the same rules and regulations as other WTO members. China's accession to the organization in 2001 should have alleviated much of this concern, yet there are constant reports that the country does not hold itself to many of the WTO's principles—namely, a free-floating fiat currency, low tariffs, free markets, environmental standards, labor protections, and product safety/quality.

In 2015, the United States had a trade deficit with China of $365 billion, the largest bilateral deficit in the world by far.[10] Although the United States' negative trade balance is not new (it held negative balances with Germany and Japan throughout much of the twentieth century), the scale and depth of its negative trade dynamic with China is unique. China is able to maintain a positive trade balance with the United States by it keeping its exchange rate artificially low, which boosts exports by making them cheaper (and therefore more competitive), while it limits imports by instituting higher tariffs. It has also been accused of "dumping products" (putting products on the market for prices so low that it causes other nations' companies to go out of business). By engaging in this practice, their companies are able to gain a monopoly of the market share.

High tariffs and protectionist policies exacerbate the trade deficit and make it harder for US producers to penetrate the Chinese market. American tech companies such as Facebook, Amazon, and Google have tried and failed wholesale in their attempts at tapping into this market, as their cloned counterparts, named Renren, Alibaba, and Baidu, have a monopoly on social media, search, and e-commerce. Tech isn't the only area where there is robust Chinese protectionism, as their tariffs on US-produced autos are 25 percent, while US duties on imports hover around 5 percent.[11] By having

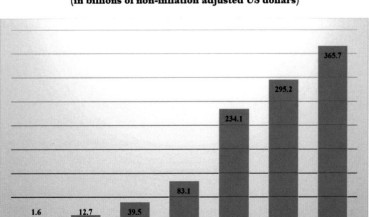

Chart 23
US TRADE DEFICIT WITH CHINA, 1986–2015
(in billions of non-inflation adjusted US dollars)

high tariffs on imports (which drives up the price of these products), Chinese-built cars/products are therefore cheaper and enjoy an unfair advantage. China has taken advantage of the United States' free trade and low barriers of entry to its consuming class and has embraced the policy of mercantilism—the deliberate gaming of the international system by way of protectionism and state capitalism. Because of these policies, there has been a domestic call by several politicians (most notably Donald Trump) for a populist/protectionist approach to our trade deals with China—typically in the form of indiscriminatingly slapping tariffs on all Chinese goods—which would trigger a trade war with no winners.

Note: As an ardently capitalist and free-trading nation, the United States typically has lower tariffs on many goods and has a lower barrier to entry than most nations it trades with. This is why Volkswagens (made by Germany), Hyundais (made by Korea), and Toyotas (made by Japan) are ubiquitous on American highways, yet the inverse is seldom true.

The last issue of note is China's deliberate attempts at hacking into our computer systems, especially in the defense and government realms. These attacks allow the Chinese to save huge sums of money in investing, research, and development and also put our national security at risk. In 2014, a Chinese citizen and owner of an aviation-technology company was caught with sixty-five gigabytes of data from Boeing and allegedly sought data from Lockheed Martin's F-22 and F-35 fighter jets, both of which the United States spent tens of billions of dollars developing.[12] China has proven to be adept at soliciting/extracting data from sympathetic expatriates or engaging in asymmetric warfare by entire units within its People's Liberation Army (PLA) in order to close the technology gap with the United States. Listed here are some examples of the strategy that these units are engaging in:

In 2014, a grand jury indicted five Chinese military hackers for economic espionage directed at American targets in the nuclear power, metals, and solar products industries. "This case represents the first ever charges against a state actor for this type of hacking," US Attorney General Eric Holder said. "The range of trade secrets and other sensitive business information stolen in this case is significant. Success in the global marketplace should be based solely on a company's ability to innovate and compete, not on a sponsor government's ability to spy and steal business secrets."[13]

China has essentially divided its cyber warfare forces into three components. First, there are what the Chinese call "specialized military network warfare forces," consisting of operational military units employed for carrying out network attack and defense. Second, China has teams of specialists in civilian organizations that have been authorized by the military to carry out network warfare operations. Those civilian organizations include the Ministry of State Security, which is essentially China's version of the CIA, and the Ministry of Public Security (its FBI). Finally, there are "external entities" outside the government that can be organized and mobilized for network warfare operations.[14]

This chapter discussed the many areas in which the United States and China stand in opposition, a contrast to the economic codependence discussed in chapter 6. The next chapter will theorize and predict how long this marriage of convenience will last and whether the ties that bind are more robust than the potential for friction.

Chapter 8

WHAT DOES THIS RELATIONSHIP LOOK LIKE IN THE FUTURE?

It is a perilous game to make predictions about future bilateral relations between these two nations since so many factors (political, economic, military) are at play. However, based on current geopolitical and economic trends, I feel confident making four general hypotheses about what the next few decades of Chimerica (an oft-used description in foreign policy circles) might look like:

1. America and China will become more powerful as an economic unit (the G-2).
2. Their large amount of bilateral trade will temper the prospect of war.
3. Both nations will engage in strategic posturing on occasion, yet it should not lead to conflict.
4. China will look to supplant and eventually upend the US-dominated post–World War II institutional construct.

Hypothesis 1

America and China will solidify their economic positions, and their global clout will increase when compared to the traditional world powers (Europe/Japan). Global economic power will also become decentralized as the "Rise of the Rest" continues in earnest.

The following charts depict that economic power will become increasingly concentrated at the top (United States and China) when compared to the G-7 nations that were the nineteenth and twentieth centuries' traditional economic powerhouses. And although power will be "top heavy," the rise of the emerging market economies will also decentralize power and give formerly poor countries a larger say in international affairs.[1]

By referencing Charts 8.1, 8.2 and 8.3, we can make some observations with respect to global economic trends and shifts: The days of the EU and Japan's position at the pinnacle of the economic pyramid are numbered. They are not in absolute decline but are rather experiencing "relative decline," whereby emerging market nations will begin to reach economic parity in the coming decades. The EU combined for 34 percent of global GDP in 2010, yet only eleven years later, this number is slated to drop to just 25 percent.[2] Of note is India, oft regarded as the "next China," with

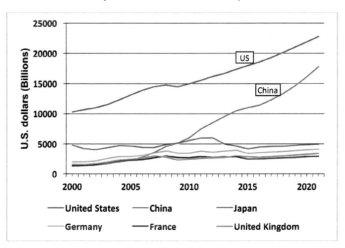

Chart 24
G-7 NATIONS AND CHINA GDP, 2000–2021
(measured in 2015 US Dollars)

Chart 25

GROSS DOMESTIC PRODUCT (GDP), 2010
(measured in 2015 US Dollars)

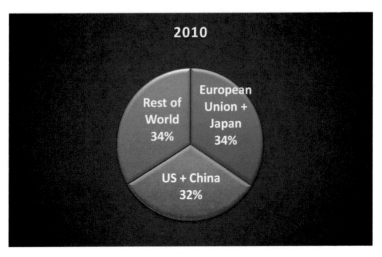

Chart 26

PREDICTED GROSS DOMESTIC PRODUCT (GDP), 2021

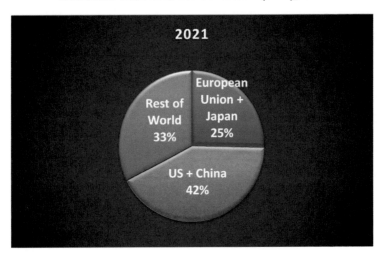

its huge untapped population of 1.32 billion people. From 2010 to 2021, India is projected to pass (in order) Italy, France, and the United Kingdom in economic size (see chart on next page). As a

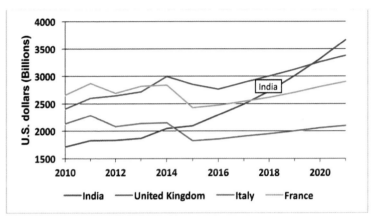

Chart 27
SELECT NATIONS' GROSS DOMESTIC PRODUCT (GDP), 2010 TO 2021
(measured in 2015 US Dollars)

former colony and client state of the British, it would have been previously unfathomable to even consider these two nations as economic peers, let alone India being larger.

The United States and China will solidify their position at the top of the global economic spectrum. From 2010 to 2021, the United States' economy, as a share of global GDP, will remain stable at roughly 23 percent, while China's share is slated to double from 9 percent to just over 18 percent. Combined, these two juggernauts will make up a whopping 42 percent of global economic output by that time. To grasp the gravity of this shift, just consider that in 1990, China's economy was just one-third size of Germany's, yet by 2021, it will be four times the size of the Fatherland.[3]

Hypothesis 2

The largesse of their bilateral trade will have a calming effect on their political relationship. America and China are at opposite ends of the spectrum when it comes to many ideological and geopolitical issues. One nation is a liberal and open democratic republic, while the other has been ruled by the Communist Party since 1950. As mentioned previously, the United States is party to several security pacts in Asia; it has active security treaties with Korea, Japan, Taiwan, and the Philippines—all of which rankle the Chinese. Similarly, the Chinese keep the North Korean state afloat by offering it loans, military hardware, and political cover in the UN, which hampers the United States' efforts at reigning in the Jong Un government. With all of these dynamics at play, the odds should lean toward conflict, but the necessity for stable markets provide respite for the near to medium term. By observing the 2009 Greek debt crisis, it is clear that stock markets and businesses abhor any situation that disrupts the natural flow of money, goods, and services. Greece has an economy of just $150 billion, which is roughly equal to the economic output of Kansas (hardly the United States' economic engine). Yet in an instant, it was able to rattle world stock markets, costing investors hundreds of billions of dollars as it spread its contagion to several other European nations. Collectively, these debt-laden European nations were known as PIIGS (Portugal, Italy, Ireland, Greece, and Spain). If a nation such as Greece—which is barely a blip on the global economic map—was able to cause such chaos, one could imagine what kind of economic armageddon would take place if one-third of the world economy (United States and China) were involved in conflict. The United States and China are involved in this century's version of Mutual Assured Destruction (MAD) in the economic realm. Just as the United States and the USSR enjoyed relative stability simply because both nations knew direct military conflict would destroy them both, the United States and China realize that the economic well-being of their respective nations and the world at large rely on peace and stability.

Hypothesis 3

Both nations' governments will posture from time to time, and there may be several moments of sheer terror, but outright war will not come to fruition (at least not in the next decade or two).

Chapter 6 talked extensively about how the increased trade between these two nations is a symbiotic dynamic whereby both parties benefit, albeit in different ways. However, that does not mean that there are none who suffer from this relationship, evidenced by the millions of US workers in the manufacturing sector whose jobs were replaced with cheaper overseas labor. One only has to watch a few minutes of a US politician's speech on trade before the words "globalization, China, TPP, and NAFTA" are brought up in a pejorative manner. Americans are proud (and rightly so) of their industrial past, as Made in America used to be a source of pride for our manufacturing sector. The obvious scapegoat for those wishing for the return to yesteryear is low-cost competition overseas (the biggest of which is China). Since it is a country that many Americans know little about besides that line that "they're taking our jobs," it is the inevitable low-hanging fruit for those wishing to score easy political points, especially in the Rust Belt states.

For its part, the Chinese government is adept at making the United States a target of its ire, and through its government-run media outlets, the Chinese routinely deride America and paint it in a negative light. But while the United States' angst toward China is primarily driven by economics, China's assertions are centered on America's foreign policy and military actions in the Pacific. It fears that the United States is encircling it through military alliances and naval deployments and is trying to stifle Chinese influence in the region. From the Taiwan issue to the disputed islands in the South/East China Seas, it views America as meddling in the affairs of its rightful sphere of influence. Blaming the United States also acts as a release valve for its citizens while increasing national pride and support for the Communist regime.

Many of these acts on both sides can be chalked up to geopolitical posturing, whereby a rival makes statements strictly to illicit a specific response. Secretary Kissinger's legacy of Realpolitik—Machiavellian-based power politics centered on real-time facts on the ground that are not formed by ideology—will frame this bilateral relationship. Foreign policy is a strategic discipline in which each nation-state is constantly trying to improve its position through cunning; it is a game of chess on a massive scale. That being said, there are times that the anticipated response or action does not fall in line with a nation's calculations, causing situations to snowball and intensify beyond control, which is how many conflicts have unintentionally commenced throughout history. Although I do feel the likelihood of Sino-American conflict is low, let's play out how a future conflict could look and then assess who would be the winners and losers in this potential scenario.

July 15, 2021: There are rumors of a popular uprising being planned to overthrow the Communist government in China, as its ever-expanding middle class has been consistently protesting for more freedoms and rights—with only token concessions made by the government. Furthermore, there is a recession on the mainland, causing its citizens to have less patience with the politburo. The Communist government blames the United States and neighboring Asian nations for unfair trade practices, which it claims exacerbated the recession. In an attempt to restore national pride and take the citizens' focus off the government's failings, the Chinese president declares in the state-run paper, China Daily, that any nation (including the United States) found operating near the South China Sea's disputed islands will be dealt with swiftly and that any intrusion on China's territorial sovereignty will not be tolerated.

July 25, 2021: To show the seriousness of their territorial pronouncements, the Chinese military detains a Taiwanese military vessel and a Vietnamese fishing boat for "illegal operations" in its Exclusive Economic Zone (EEZ) around the Spratly Islands in the South China Sea.

July 30, 2021: To further show its displeasure with Taiwan, China holds aggressive military exercises in the Taiwan Strait and shoots munitions just off the coast of Taiwan. One of its artillery shells from the military exercises goes astray and kills five Taiwan citizens. Responding to China's military overtures and a recent surge in nationalist sentiment, the Taiwanese president publicly calls for a nationwide referendum on the possibility of declaring formal independence from the mainland.

July 31, 2021: A Chinese Chengdu J-10 shoots down a Taiwanese reconnaissance plane it says was operating over its airspace, but in reality, it was a warning for the Taiwanese to lessen their rhetoric on declaring independence.

July 31, 2021: The United States publicly denounces China's actions and calls for an emergency UN Security Council Meeting.

August 2, 2021: The Association of Southeast Asian Nations (ASEAN) also holds an emergency summit. At the summit, Brunei, Malaysia, the Philippines, Taiwan, Indonesia, and Vietnam agree to show solidarity and form a collective security alliance against China over its recent actions.

August 4, 2021: In response to this newly made alliance, one of China's sleeper agents in Taiwan assassinates the Taiwanese president and its foreign affairs minister. Hours later—as the country is still in a state of panic—the Taiwanese military takes control of the country in order to protect it from further aggression. Sensing an opportunity to reabsorb Taiwan as the island descends into chaos, China sends in three brigades of paratroopers and special forces to secure the capital and cause further havoc. It also bombs Taiwan's main command and control (C2) centers.

August 5, 2021: The United States sends two aircraft carriers to the region and gives China seventy-two hours to vacate Taiwan. The United States, the European Union, Japan, and South Korea place a trade embargo on China and do not allow any cargo ships to leave the region. World stock markets plummet, wiping away trillions of dollars overnight. No US or Chinese company is spared, as the US S&P 500 decreases by 25 percent, and the embargo pummels the Shanghai composite index, dropping it 40 percent—evaporating citizens' pensions and fomenting mass protests. Trade has halted, and every Multinational Corporation (MNC) is in a state of panic. In an effort to protect US banks from the contagion, the US Treasury and Federal Reserve have placed a twenty-four-hour restriction on bank withdrawals. Two of America's banking giants, JP Morgan and Citigroup, declare bankruptcy the following day as their overleveraged balance sheets spook investors.

August 7, 2021: China knows it needs to settle this dispute soon, as the United States' seventy-two-hour ultimatum is coming due and there are still widespread grumblings of a domestic revolution to overthrow the Communist government—the mainland's incursion into Taiwan only fanned the revolutionary flames. The United States also needs this issue settled, as there is mass pressure from Wall

Street and the president's economic advisors, who are predicting a second Great Depression should this issue not be resolved. US ten-year treasury bond rates have jumped tenfold to 30 percent, causing the United States to suspend government spending and borrowing. Through tense backdoor negotiations in the seventy-first hour, an agreement has been made: China will vacate the island, and the pre-hostility status quo with respect to Taiwan will be maintained. In reciprocation, the US Navy will redeploy its 7th Fleet back to the United States from Japan for a period of three years.

In the aftermath of the incident, there is a two-year global recession and a deep contraction in China, the United States, and Taiwan—all of which experience negative 10 percent GDP growth for several years. Across the globe, tariffs increase, trade decreases, and many nations have elected strongmen who are rife with protectionist rhetoric.

One can plainly see that there are no winners in this fictional tale, and any perceived gains would be "Pyrrhic victories" in their purest form: King Pyrrhus defeated the Romans in battle in 280 BC, yet sustained such casualties to his own forces that his armies were comprehensively gutted, causing him to state, "If we are victorious in one more battle with the Romans, we shall be utterly ruined."[4] The perceived "win" of any potential Sino-American battle would be overshadowed by the profound and systemic negative outcomes that would manifest thereafter. Furthermore, no shots were actually fired in this fictional scenario, and there were still massive global consequences. We can only image how much greater the scale of these repercussions would be if these belligerents actually met in the field of battle.

Hypothesis 4

As China and other emerging markets gain economic strength, they will look to challenge the US-led institutional order.

Many of the organizations that govern international order, economics, and security are outdated relics of a post–World War

II era that have not changed in the past seventy years. For example, the United Nations Security Council—which is responsible for ensuring international peace and security, settling disputes, and voting on the legality of inter-state conflict—is still composed of the five World War II victors (United States, China, United Kingdom, France, and Russia). As such, it is acknowledged as the preeminent security council on the planet, yet it excludes several nations that deserve a seat at the table, while it includes those who were simply on the winning side of a war fought generations ago. For example, Germany is the de facto leader of Europe, the economic engine on the continent, enjoys vast international legitimacy, and has an economy one-third larger than France's, yet it is not afforded council membership because of its role in World War II. Similarly, Japan was the world's second-largest economy for most of the postwar era and has an economy *four times* the size of Russia's, yet it similarly is not a member of the council. Furthermore, no nation from Central/South America, Eastern Europe, or the Middle East is represented. Charts 28 and 29 how ill-represented this council is, leaving out many of the world's richest nations (Japan, Germany), as well as some of its most populous (India, Brazil).[5]

The UN, World Bank, IMF, and the establishment of the US dollar as the world's reserve currency were all borne out of the ashes of World War II, and it will likely take another global catastrophic event for these constructs to change. Since the prospect of another war enveloping the major nations of the world and wiping out

Chart 28

THE FIVE PERMANENT MEMBERS OF THE UN SECURITY COUNCIL

Nation	Economic Rank	Population Rank
United States	1	3
China	2	1
United Kingdom	5	22
France	6	21
Russia	11	9

Chart 29
NON-MEMBERS OF THE UN SECURITY COUNCIL

Nation	Economic Rank	Population Rank
Japan	3	11
Germany	4	16
Brazil	7	5
India	9	2

Note: there are ten non-permanent members of this council that do represent different regions of the world, yet they serve only for two-year terms before being rotated out.

the entire international order apparatus in the process is a rather slim prospect, China, the BRICS (Brazil, Russia, India, and South Africa), and other emerging market nations are attempting other means to encroach on the West's dominance. One of their strategies involves the pooling of economic resources in order to lessen the need for dollar dependency.

In July 2014, Russia, Brazil, India, China, and South Africa were signatories to a reserve currency pool worth over $100 billion that will give BRICS member states opportunity outside of the World Bank/IMF system to provide one another with financial assistance in case of problems with their balance of payments.[6]

Beijing govenor Zhou Xiaochuan noted, "The world economic crisis shows the 'inherent vulnerabilities and systemic risks in the existing international monetary system.' Creating a currency made up of a basket of global currencies and controlled by the IMF would help to achieve the objective of safeguarding global economic and financial stability."[7] These increasing calls by China and Russia for an introduction of a basket of currencies called Special Drawing Rights (SDRs) is a plan that might eventually attempt to supplant the US dollar as the global reserve currency.

Chinese economics researcher Yi Xianrong notes, "Proper representation and a bigger voice for the emerging developing countries are the need of the hour. For instance, being the world's second-largest economy and the largest foreign reserves holder, China should get its due place in the monetary body."[8]

These calls for monetary change by emerging market nations have not had much practical effect in the near term, yet this is of nominal importance. What matters is that these rumblings for change in the economic realm are manifesting in the first place, rumblings that might become more fervent and could potentially spread into a globally galvanizing cause.

At some point, the West will have to come to terms with the coming power shift in economics and especially demographics. By 2050, Nigeria alone will have twice as many people as the combined totals of France, England, and Germany.[9] Almost every single Western nation is in terminal demographic decline—by 2050, the United States will be the lone member of NATO and the G-7 in the rankings of the fifteen most populous countries on earth. There will also be zero European nations on this list, with its most populous country (United Kingdom) ranked as number twenty-four. How the United States and the West deal with these startling demographic projections will be of crucial importance. As most of the members of

Chart 30
FIFTEEN MOST POPULOUS COUNTRIES, 2050

Nation	Population (in billions)	Member of NATO?	Member of G-7?
India	1,700	No	No
China	1,33	No	No
Nigeria	398	No	No
United States	*385*	*Yes*	*Yes*
Indonesia	322	No	No
Pakistan	309	No	No
Brazil	238	No	No
Bangladesh	202	No	No
Congo, Dem. Rep.	195	No	No
Ethiopia	188	No	No
Mexico	163	No	No
Egypt	151	No	No
Philippines	148	No	No
Tanzania	137	No	No
Russia	128	No	No

the chart on page 87 are emerging market economies, conventional wisdom would dictate that they would be more aligned with China on a myriad of issues, including labor and product regulations, human rights, and trade. As demographic advantages are exploited and emerging market economies reach economic parity (and eventually surpass) the traditional Western powers in terms of GDP, political conflict might arise. Developing nations will want a larger say in multinational institutions, yet Western nations will not want to voluntarily cede power, even though they ostensibly should.[10]

CONCLUSION

The United States has had the world's largest economy for over 125 years unbroken. With only 4 percent of the world's population, it has garnered 20 to 30 percent of global GDP for the past seven decades, owing to its dynamic and capitalist-based economy, entrepreneurism, ability to be a magnet for the world's best and brightest, and lots of luck. Luck is mentioned for several reasons:

1. The United States' enviable location, void of any potential belligerents and flanked by two large oceans, which act as mammoth moats against invaders.
2. The United States was the only major industrialized nation spared from the awesome destruction from two global wars that shattered entire economies. Out of the 100 million people killed during these wars, the United States incurred only 0.5 percent of the causalities (roughly 500,000 men).[1]
3. The United States is one of the only nations throughout history to be bestowed as the global leader in a bloodless transition of power. The British ceded global hegemony after World War II for an enduring seat at the table in a new US-led order, which began the US-UK "Special Relationship."

It must be acknowledged that globalization, technological diffusion, the exchange of people and ideas, and the "Rise of the Rest" are eroding much of these fortunate circumstances. The United States' unchallenged dominance was/is an unnatural situation that will inevitably return to homeostasis at some point. As mentioned in the introduction, IMF estimates show that within the next ten to fifteen years, China will displace the United States as the world's largest economy. With 1.38 billion citizens and 20 percent of the world's population, it *should* hold that position. What will matter is how China and the United States treat this very unusual dynamic, whereby China has the world's largest economy in terms of gross output yet will still be considered a developing nation that lags behind the United States in the other three components that compose national power (military, political, and soft power).

Although it will be smaller in GDP, the United States should keep its position as the world's most dynamic and modern economy so long as it maintains its unique recipe for success, which revolves around openness, free trade, and liberal immigration policies. As a heterogeneous nation without a defined ethnic anchor (German being its largest ethnic contributor, with over forty-six million descendants), the United States is not a nation-state in the traditional sense.[2] Its lack of national ethnicity and its open, liberal society are several reasons it is able to seamlessly absorb millions of immigrants, who study science, technology, engineering, and mathematics (STEM) in much higher numbers than domestic-born students. This entrepreneurial and tech-focused cohort is a crucial reason behind the United States' scientific primacy, as over half of all Silicon Valley startups worth over $1 billion in assets were founded by immigrants.[3]

Tech leaders, including Mark Zuckerberg and Bill Gates, have called for increasing the number of H-1B visas that let skilled foreign workers stay in the country. They argue that immigration greatly benefits the tech community and that it is difficult for companies to hire foreign-born workers and for immigrant entrepreneurs to start businesses due to the visas' constraints.[4]

Conversely, I feel that China's lack of immigration limits its ability to challenge the United States, for it can draw only on its 1.38 billion domestic citizens as engines for economic growth, while the United States can draw on the more than 7 billion global citizens (including the millions of Chinese who have successfully immigrated to the States). In fact, once Chinese citizens attain the means to emigrate, they tend to do so in large numbers: 10 million Chinese have flowed outside of the country's borders since 1978—the largest exodus of any nation in that timeframe.[5] Of these 10 million, the most common destination has been America, where they have contributed to America's economic strength in very concrete terms.

In contrast to America's melting-pot society, China's priority for ethnic homogeneity is a drag on its potential and is a policy that is unlikely to change. It is built into the Chinese societal fabric, as evidenced by Amy Chua's depiction in her book Day of Empire:

> *As a child, one of the first things I learned was the difference between a Han Chinese person and everyone else. It went without saying that being Han was not something that could be learned or acquired through acculturation. A white person—no matter how fluent in Chinese, no matter how long he had lived in China—could never be Han. My mother spoke frequently of the magnificence of China's 5,000-year history and the superiority of Chinese culture. She also talked about the "purity" of Chinese blood and what a shame it would be to dilute it. In my native dialect, the height of insult is to describe someone as tzup jerg—literally "of ten breeds"; the closest English equivalent is probably mongrel.[6]*

China will likely stay several decades behind the United States in terms of global military reach, as it is unlikely that China will have the ability to achieve anything close to the United States' global-basing apparatus. The "benign hegemon" was able to attain many of its basing rights from its role in the major wars of the twentieth century (World War II, Korea, Desert Storm), and most of these nations prefer that these troops stay, as the US military provides for their national security and saves them billions of defense dollars. For all of its blunders on the global stage, the United States is still trusted the world over and is not generally perceived as a threat to use these bases as staging grounds for imperial ambitions. Conversely, many nations view China's rise with skepticism and are unaware how it will act once it achieves great power status, so it is unlikely that a string of overseas bases outside the mainland will manifest.

With respect to technology, China is still getting its feet wet with many systems the United States has been operating for several decades. For example, China is in the midst of launching its first aircraft carrier—a complex floating military base that takes years to learn how to properly deploy, maintain, and utilize in a real-world combat environment. While China's first carrier will not be combat ready for several years, in 2016, the United States launched its seventy-eighth carrier (the USS Gerald R Ford) and has been using them for almost a century. The United States also enjoys a technological buffer of a decade or more with respect to many advanced military systems, especially in the stealth aircraft; missile defense; and intelligence, reconnaissance, surveillance (ISR) arenas.

There is broad international consensus that the United States should maintain its leading role in many political institutions. It is the center of gravity in the UN Security Council, World Bank, IMF, NATO, and WTO. It is bound through mutual-defense treaties with Korea, Taiwan, Japan, Australia, and the Philippines, all of which are within China's sphere of influence and therefore can be used as a means to shape China's ascent. China's only major agreements are an aid and cooperation treaty with North Korea and a twenty-year "Treaty of Friendship" agreement signed with Russia in 2001. Both North Korea and Russia are international pariahs at the moment, so these informal alliances' ability to sway international sentiment is limited. Conversely, the United States' web of international military alliances encompasses over half of global GDP, affording it vast means to influence global dynamics.[7]

American ideas, popular culture, and large ethnic diasporas supply the United States with large amounts of soft power and international goodwill. Although specific American policies might have been derided globally (such as the wars in Vietnam and Iraq), citizens generally have a positive view of Americans and what the country purportedly stands for. Over forty-six million immigrants live in the United States, amounting to 20 percent of all global immigrants.[8] If US immigrants were their own nation, it would outrank nearly 170 countries in total population, with more people than Poland.[9] While traveling across the globe in my career in the US Army, it seemed that everyone "had a cousin in the States," and most had positive anecdotes—whether it be reminiscing about watching John Wayne movies as a youngster or recalling how devastated they were when Kennedy was shot. People are hard-pressed to harbor negative sentiments toward a country in which he or she has relatives living, whose prominent culture (music, movies, brands, restaurants) surrounds them, is the largest donor of international aid, and leads a liberal world order that encourages openness and individual liberties. In short, people are comfortable with American leadership, for it is leadership they know and can trust. Conversely, there is much more anxiety about what a potential Chinese-led world order would look like.

It is my belief that xenophobic rhetoric, closing itself off from globalization, and stymying outside forces—whether it be trade, people, or ideas—is the only way America's future would become darker and less prosperous.

Like every world-dominant power before it, the United States is a hyperpower today because it has surpassed all its rivals in pulling in and motivating the world's most valuable human capital. Turning its back on immigration would destroy the very underpinnings of its prosperity and preeminence at a time when, in the words of Google vice president Laszlo Bock, "we are in a fierce worldwide competition for top talent unlike ever before." The destructive effects of anti-immigration policies might be felt sooner than Americans realize. Microsoft founder Bill Gates recently testified before a US Senate committee that the United States' post-9/11 immigration measures are "driving away the world's best and brightest precisely when we need them most."[10]

Throughout history, the prospect for war has been greatest when the status quo power (in this case, the United States) is viewed as declining, while the rising power (China) is viewed as challenging the hegemon and the global order over which it presides. It is my estimation that in the medium term (two to three decades), China cannot become a global hegemon in the same vein as the United States. The United States' position as the keeper of global order is costly, and China would prefer to grow economically and modernize under the stability the United States and the West provide without having to devote considerable resources to ensure the viability of this system. It may have some regional ambitions (Taiwan and the South/East China Seas disputes), which should be issues of note for the United States, but the prospects of China wanting to create an independent new world order outside the current construct are slim. The United States became the world's largest economy in the 1890s, and it took over fifty years for that economic power to translate to military and institutional power, whereby it displaced the European powers following World War II. Had it not been for that catastrophic global event, it might have taken the United States another several decades or more to assume its preeminent global position. It is therefore prudent to assume that even when China's economy does outstrip the United States', it will likely take many decades for it to challenge the States in other areas, especially ones around which America has constructed large moats.

It is my assessment that both the United States and China have very bright futures ahead of them, so long as they stay consistent with the respective recipes that have made them successful. For America, it is ensuring that its open and liberal economic and immigration policies allow entrepreneurial activity to thrive, keeping it at the cutting edge of innovation. China's future is a bit more convoluted, as the Communist Party must eventually address how to give its burgeoning middle class more freedom without losing its dominance as the country's lone political party. Both of these happenings can take place within a broader context of peaceful bilateral relations as long as the ambitions and aspirations of each are clearly defined and understood by their counterpart.

In summation, let me leave you with this: The United States and China are not allies in the traditional sense and have few cultural, military, ideological, religious, or historic links that tend to bind traditional alliances. Yet we exchange money and goods—lots of both. For that reason, we have a marriage of convenience, for better or worse, till death do us part.

NOTES

Chapter 1

1. United States Census Bureau, "Foreign Trade: Trade in Goods with China," https://www.census.gov/foreign-trade/balance/c5700.html.
2. Knoema, "IMF World Economic Outlook (WEO), April 2016," https://knoema.com/IMFWEO2016Apr/imf-world-economic-outlook-weo-april-2016.
3. "The Collapse of the Soviet Union and Ronald Reagan," http://wais.stanford.edu/History/history_ussrandreagan.htm. Chart 1 is from IIP Digital, "Why the Stockpiles?" http://iipdigital.usembassy.gov/st/english/publication/2010/02/20100222190335ebyessedo3.511554e-02.html#axzz492JiwfDK

Chapter 2

1. Iain Haddow, "When UK GDP Last Outstripped the US," BBC News, http://news.bbc.co.uk/2/hi/uk_news/7174996.stm.
2. United States Census Bureau, "Foreign Trade: Top Trading Partners—December 2015," https://www.census.gov/foreign-trade/statistics/highlights/top/top1512yr.html.

3. Amy Chua, *Day of Empire* (New York: First Anchor Books, 2007).

4. Elgin Groseclose, *America's Money Machine: The Story of the Federal Reserves* (Auburn, AL: Ludwig von Mises Institute, 2009), available online at Google Books.

5. Time Toast, "Non-Interventionism in America," https://www.timetoast.com/timelines/non-interventionism-in-america

6. *New York Times*, "The Monroe Doctrine," July 4, 1865, http://www.nytimes.com/1865/07/04/news/monroe-doctrine-political-circumstances-under-which-it-was-enunciated-french.html?pagewanted=all

7. The Commonwealth, "Member Countries," http://thecommonwealth.org/member-countries.

8. Valerie Hansen, *The Open Empire: A History of China to 1600* (New York: W.W. Norton & Co., 2000).

9. Caroylyn Marvin, "'All Under Heaven'—Megaspace in Beijing," in *Owning the Olympics*, edited by M.E. Price and D. Dayan, pp. 229–259 (Ann Arbor: University of Michigan Press and the University of Michigan, 2008), http://repository.upenn.edu/asc_papers/127.

10. War Chronicle, "Estimated War Dead: World War II," http://warchronicle.com/numbers/WWII/deaths.htm.

Chapter 3

1. Tony Rennell, "Madman Who Starved 60 Million to Death," Daily Mail, http://www.dailymail.co.uk/news/article-2017839/Madman-starved-60-million-death-Devastating-book-reveals-Maos-megalomania-turned-China-madhouse.html.

2. History Learning Site, "The Great Leap Forward," http://www.historylearningsite.co.uk/modern-world-history-1918-to-1980/china-1900-to-1976/the-great-leap-forward.

3. Newark College of Arts and Sciences, "Mao and The Great Leap Forward," Rutgers, http://www.ncas.rutgers.edu/mao-and-great-leap-forward.

5. History, "Cultural Revolution," http://www.history.com/topics/cultural-revolution.

6. Brainy Quote, "Deng Xiaoping Quotes," http://www. brainyquote.com/quotes/authors/d/deng_xiaoping.html.
7. Bureau of Economic Analysis, "Industry Data," http:// www.bea. gov/iTable/index_industry_gdpindy.cfm.
8. World Bank, "World Development Indicators," http:// databank. worldbank.org/data/reports.aspx? source=2&country=CHN&se ries=&period.
9. International Economics Study Center, "Chapter 5: WTO Accession," http://internationalecon.com/wto/ch5.php.

Chapter 4

1. Knoema, "IMF World Economic Outlook (WEO), April 2016," https://knoema.com/IMFWEO2016Apr/imf-world-economic-outlook-weo-april-2016.
2. Ibid.
3. Trading Economics, "China Annual Growth Rate," http://www. tradingeconomics.com/china/gdp-growth-annual.
4. World Bank, "GDP Per Capita (Current US$)," http://data. worldbank.org/indicator/NY.GDP.PCAP.CD.
5. Central Intelligence Agency, "The World Fact Book," https:// www.cia.gov/library/publications/the-world-factbook/ rankorder/2003rank.html#zi.
6. Trading Economics, "China Annual Growth Rate"; China Daily, "China's Poverty Cut Off Too Low," http://usa.chinadaily.com. cn/business/2014-09/09/content_18569778.htm; International Business Times, "China: More than 82 Million People Live Below Poverty Line," http://www.ibtimes.co.uk/china-more-82- million-people-live-below-poverty-line-1470313.
7. Demographia, "US Population from 1900," http://www. demographia.com/db-uspop1900.htm.
8. Trading Economics, "India GDP per Capita," http://www. tradingeconomics.com/india/gdp-per-capita.
9. Trans-Canada, "TransCanada Challenges Keystone XL Denial," http://www.keystone-xl.com.

10. Worldometers, "Countries in the World by Population (2016)," http://www.worldometers.info/world-population/population-by-country.

11. "Real Historical Gross Domestic Product for Baseline Countries/ Regions (in percent) 1969–2014," http://ers.usda.gov/datafiles/ International_Macroeconomic_Data/Historical_Data_Files/ HistoricalGDPSharesValues.xls.

12. Knoema, "GDP per Capita by Country 1980–2014," https:// knoema.com/pjeqzh/gdp-per-capita-by-country-1980-2014?country=United%20States.

13. Chart 6 available online.

Chapter 5

1. *New York Times*, "To Paris, US Looks Like a 'Hyperpower,'" February 5, 1999, http://www.nytimes.com/1999/02/05/ news/05iht-france.t_0.html.

2. Worldometers, "Countries in the World by Population (2016),"http://www.worldometers.info/world-population/ population-by-country.

3. *New York Times*, "To Paris."

4. Charts 7 and 8: *New York Times*, "To Paris"; Dogs of the Dow, "Largest Companies by Market Cap Today," http:// dogsofthedow.com/largest-companies-by-market-cap.htm; Market Watch, "Here's the Map of the World, if Size Were Determined by Market Cap," http://www.marketwatch.com/ story/heres-the-map-of-the-world-if-size-was-determined-by-market-cap-2015-08-12.

5. Times Higher Education, "World University Rankings," https://www.timeshighereducation.com/world-university-rankings/2016/world-ranking#!/page/0/length/25/sort_by/ rank_label/sort_order/asc/cols/rank_only.

6. Marc Auboin, "Use of Currencies in International Trade: Any Changes in the Picture?" World Trade Organization, "https:// www.wto.org/english/res_e/reser_e/ersd201210_e.pdf.

7. Global Finance, "Composition of Foreign Exchange Reserves 2015," https://www.gfmag.com/global-data/economic-data/economic-dataforeign-exchange-reserves?page=2.

8. Ibid.; Chart 11: https://cointelegraph.com/news/rumor-mill-new-reserve-currency-may-rock-us-dollar-in-october.

9. Market Watch, "Here's the Map of the World, if Size Were Determined by Market Cap," http://www.marketwatch.com/story/heres-the-map-of-the-world-if-size-was-determined-by-market-cap-2015-08-12

10. David Vine, "Where in the World Is the US Military?" *Politico Magazine*, July/August 2015, http://www.politico.com/magazine/story/2015/06/us-military-bases-around-the-world-119321; Graphics, "This Graphic Shows Where U.S. Troops Are Stationed Around the World," http://time.com/4075458/afghanistan-drawdown-obama-troops.

11. David Vine, "The United States Probably Has More Foreign Military Bases Than Any Other People, Nation, or Empire in History," *Nation*, September 14, 2015, https://www.thenation.com/article/the-united-states-probably-has-more-foreign-military-bases-than-any-other-people-nation-or-empire-in-history; Patrick Winn, "Five Expensive US Military Bases Spark Controversy Abroad," Truthout, October 7, 2010, http://truth-out.org/archive/component/k2/item/92192:five-expensive-us-military-bases-spark-controversy-abroad; Nationmaster, "Geography: Land Area: Square Miles: Countries Compared," http://www.nationmaster.com/country-info/stats/Geography/Land-area/Square-miles.

12. Information Diet, "U.S. Troop Levels in Iraq and Afghanistan Per Year," http://theinformationdiet.blogspot.com/2011/11/us-troop-levels-in-iraq-and-afghanistan.html; *Hurriyet Daily News*, "UK Army Faces Strain if Iraq, Afghan Missions Runs On," February 5, 2006, http://www.hurriyetdailynews.com/uk-army-faces-strain-if-iraq-afghan-missions-run-on.aspx?pageID=438&n=uk-army-faces-strain-if-iraq-afghan-missions-run-on-2006-02-05.

13. Daniel R. Deakin, "The 10 Largest Combat Air Forces in the World," The Richest, http://www.therichest.com/rich-list/the-top-10-largest-combat-air-forces-in-the-world; Statista, "Total

Aircraft Force of the U.S. Navy for Fiscal Years 1995 to 2017, by Wingtype," http://www.statista.com/statistics/239324/total-aircraft-force-of-the-us-navy; 2015 Index of Military Strength, "U.S. Air Force," http://index.heritage.org/military/2015/chapter/us-power/us-air-force.

14. Jim Garamone, "Gates: Sea Services Must Question Embedded Thinking," US Department of Defense, http://archive.defense.gov/news/newsarticle.aspx?id=59000.

15. Telegraph, "Nobel Prize Winners: Which Country Has the Most Nobel Laureates?" http://www.telegraph.co.uk/news/worldnews/northamerica/usa/11926364/Nobel-Prize-winners-Which-country-has-the-most-Nobel-laureates.html.

Chapter 6

1. Travel China Guide, "Chinese Ethnic Groups," https://www.travelchinaguide.com/intro/nationality.

2. Trading Economies, "GDP," http://www.tradingeconomics.com/country-list/gdp.

3. Chart 14: Trading Economies, "GDP"; Television History: The First 75 Years, "TV Selling Prices," http://www.tvhistory.tv/tv-prices.htm.

4. World Bank, "Household final consumption expenditure, etc. (% of GDP)," http://data.worldbank.org/indicator/NE.CON.PETC.ZS.

5. Chart 15: Davemanuel.com, "A History of Surpluses and Deficits in the United States," http://www.davemanuel.com/history-of-deficits-and-surpluses-in-the-united-states.php.

6. Louis D. Johnson, "History Lessons: Understanding the Decline in Manufacturing," *Minn Post*, February 22, 2012, https://www.minnpost.com/macro-micro-minnesota/2012/02/history-lessons-understanding-decline-manufacturing

7. Chart 16: Douglas W. Elmendorf and Louise Sheiner, "Persistently Low Interest Rates Argue for Delayed Budget Belt-Tightening Even in an Aging America," Brookings, February 3, 2016, https://www.brookings.edu/research/persistently-low-interest-rates-argue-for-delayed-budget-belt-tightening-even-in-an-aging-america.

8. Paul Thurrott, "Blast from the Past: Buying a Computer in 1995," Supersite Windows, December 27, 2011, http://winsupersite.com/article/commentary/blast-buying-computer-1995-141723; Television History: The First 75 Years, "TV Selling Prices."

9. Amazon.com.

10. Chart 17: Paul Thurrott, "Blast from the Past"; Television History: The First 75 Years, "TV Selling Prices"; Amazon.com.

11. United Census Bureau, "Trade in Goods with China," https://www.census.gov/foreign-trade/balance/c5700.html; Knoema, "IMF World Economic Outlook (WEO), April 2016," https://knoema.com/IMFWEO2016Apr/imf-world-economic-outlook-weo-april-2016.

12. OECD Insights, "The Most Successful Anti-Poverty Movement in History?" http://oecdinsights.org/2015/07/22/the-most-successful-anti-poverty-movement-in-history; Chart 18: United Census Bureau, "Trade in Goods with China"; Knoema, "IMF World Economic Outlook."

13. National Accounts Main Agragates Database, "Basic Data Selection," http://unstats.un.org/unsd/snaama/selbasicFast.asp.

14. Trading Economics, "Chinese Yaun, 1981–2016: US Day of Reckoning," http://money.cnn.com/2016/05/10/news/economy/us-debt-ownership.

15. DaveManuel.com, "A History of Surpluses and Deficits in the United States," http://www.davemanuel.com/history-of-deficits-and-surpluses-in-the-united-states.php.

16. Heather Long, "Who Owns America's Debt?" CNNMoney.com, http://money.cnn.com/2016/05/10/news/economy/us-debt-ownership.

17. Ibid.

18. C. Fred Bergsten, "Two's Company," *Foreign Affairs*, https://www.foreignaffairs.com/articles/americas/2009-09-01/twos-company.

Chapter 7

1. Blue Marble Citizen, "Taiwan Population 1950 to 2050," http://www.bluemarblecitizen.com/world-population/Taiwan.

2. Taiwan Documents Project, "Resolution on the Restoration of the Lawful Rights of the People's Republic of China in the United Nations," http://www.taiwandocuments.org/un2758-XXVI.htm.

3. US Department of State, "US Relations with Taiwan," http://www.state.gov/r/pa/ei/bgn/35855.htm.

4. *The Guardian*, "China Warns Against First Major US-Taiwan Arms Sale in Four Years," https://www.theguardian.com/us-news/2015/dec/16/china-warns-against-us-taiwan-arms-sale-defence.

5. Central Intelligence Agency, "The World Factbook," https://www.cia.gov/library/publications/the-world-factbook/geos/kn.html.

6. Defense News, "US, Japan Strike New Military Agreement," http://www.defensenews.com/story/breaking-news/2015/04/27/us-japan-new-military-agreement/26443297.

7. Kelsey Broderick, "Chinese Activities in the South China Sea: Implications for the American Pivot to Asia," May 2015, http://www.project2049.net/documents/150511_Broderick_Chinese_Activities_South_China_Sea_Pivot.pdf.

8. Map 1: http://www.phamhongphuoc.net/wp-content/uploads/2014/05/nine-dash-line-china.jpg; Map 2: Rami Ayyub, "A Primer on the Complicated Battle for the South China Sea," npr.org, http://www.npr.org/sections/parallels/2016/04/13/472711435/a-primer-on-the-complicated-battle-for-the-south-china-sea.

9. *Daily Star*, "Not Frightened to Fight a War," http://www.thedailystar.net/world/not-frightened-fight-war-164044.

10. United States Census Bureau, "Trade in Goods with China," https://www.census.gov/foreign-trade/balance/c5700.html. See also Chart 23.

11. Baizhu Chen, "Tear Down This Wall—the Chinese Tariff Wall," *Forbes*, http://www.forbes.com/forbes/welcome/?toURL=http://www.forbes.com/sites/baizhuchen/2012/07/12/tear-down-this-wall-the-chinese-tariff-wall/&refURL=&referrer=#7e9cc87856ef.

12. Edvard Pettersson, "Chinese Hackers Allegedly Hit Boeing, Get Data on Military Planes," *Seattle Times*, July 12, 2014, http://

www.seattletimes.com/business/chinese-hackers-allegedly-hit-boeing-get-data-on-military-planes.

13. US Department of Justice, "U.S. Charges Five Chinese Military Hackers for Cyber Espionage Against U.S. Corporations and a Labor Organization for Commercial Advantage," https://www.justice.gov/opa/pr/us-charges-five-chinese-military-hackers-cyber-espionage-against-us-corporations-and-labor.

14. Shane Harris, "China Reveals Its Cyberwar Secrets," *Daily Beast*, March 18, 2015, http://www.thedailybeast.com/articles/2015/03/18/china-reveals-its-cyber-war-secrets.html.

Chapter 8

1. Knoema, "IMF World Economic Outlook (WEO), April 2016," https://knoema.com/IMFWEO2016Apr/imf-world-economic-outlook-weo-april-2016; "Total Population by Country, 1950, 2000, 2015, 2025, 2050," http://www.photius.com/rankings/world2050_rank.html.

2. Knoema, "IMF World Economic Outlook."

3. Ibid.; "Total Population by Country."

4. Wikipedia, "Pyrrhic Victory," https://en.wikipedia.org/wiki/Pyrrhic_victory#cite_note-3.

5. Knoema, "IMF World Economic Outlook"; "Total Population by Country."

6. RT Question More, "BRICS Kick Starts $100bn Reserve Currency Pool," https://www.rt.com/business/272362-brics-currency-pool-agreement.

7. Peter Koenig, "Russia and China: The Dawning of a New Monetary System?" Global Research, January 9, 2015, http://www.globalresearch.ca/russia-and-china-the-dawning-of-a-new-monetary-system/5423637.

8. Joe McDonald, "China Calls for New Global Currency," ABC News, http://abcnews.go.com/Business/story?id=7168919&page=1.

9. World Data Bank, "Health Nutrition and Population Statistics: Population Estimates and Projections," http://databank.worldbank.org/data/reports.aspx?source=Health%20Nutrition%20and%20

Population%20Statistics:%20Population%20estimates%20and%20projections#.

10. Ibid.

Conclusion

1. National WWII Museum, "By the Numbers: World-Wide Deaths," http://www.nationalww2museum.org/learn/education/for-students/ww2-history/ww2-by-the-numbers/world-wide-deaths.html?referrer=https://www.google.com.

2. Wikipedia, "Demography of the United States," https://en.wikipedia.org/wiki/Demography_of_the_United_States.

3. American Interest, "Majority of $1B Tech Companies Started by Immigrants," http://www.the-american-interest.com/2016/03/20/majority-of-1b-tech-companies-started-by-immigrants.

4. Ibid.

5. *Economist* (Italy issue), "The Long March Abroad," July 9–15, 2016, 14.

6. Chua, *Day of Empire*.

7. Knoema, "IMF World Economic Outlook (WEO), April 2016," https://knoema.com/IMFWEO2016Apr/imf-world-economic-outlook-weo-april-2016.

8. Pew Research Center, "5 Facts about the U.S. Rank in Worldwide Migration," http://www.pewresearch.org/fact-tank/2016/05/18/5-facts-about-the-u-s-rank-in-worldwide-migration.

9. Infoplease, "World's 50 Most Populous Countries: 2015," http://www.infoplease.com/world/statistics/most-populous-countries.html.

10. Chua, *Day of Empire*, 358.

Made in the USA
Lexington, KY
20 December 2019